What turns women on—

is a question that plagues many men and is certainly a favorite subject for conversation among most others.

Yet it is still not considered suitable for generalized social chitchat, nor are there too many women who are willing to discuss their very personal turn-ons in conversation even with a friend.

But it appears that, given the opportunity, women are eager to write without inhibition of their experiences and inner feelings, and in fact with a frankness that indicates it is a great relief to at last air and bring into the open their secret beefs and joys—here they do so in private letters which prove their interest in an enormous variety of broad stimulation and with even more specific attention to detail than most men are given to expressing.

"This author has something new and special to contribute to love. Clearly Chartham is head and shoulders above Reuben."
—*Chicago Daily News*

WHAT
TURNS
WOMEN
ON

Robert Chartham, Ph. D.

BALLANTINE BOOKS • NEW YORK

First Printing: February, 1974

Cover design by Larry Sutton

Printed in the United States of America

PENTHOUSE INTERNATIONAL LTD.
1560 Broadway, New York, N.Y. 10036

BALLANTINE BOOKS, INC.
201 East 50th Street, New York, N.Y. 10022

To Nancy Friday,
who crystallized my thoughts on women's sexuality
during our discussions on women's sexual fantasies,
with grateful thanks.

Contents

———✦❖✦———

Acknowledgments

The author and publishers wish to acknowledge kind permission to reprint passages and charts from Alfred C. Kinsey, et al., *Sexual Behavior in the Human Male*, copyright Paul H. Gebhard, Director, Indiana University Institute for Sex Research, Inc., published by W. B. Saunders Co., 1948; and Alfred C. Kinsey, et al., *Sexual Behavior in the Human Female*, copyright by Paul H. Gebhard, Director, Indiana University Institute for Sex Research, Inc., published by W. B. Saunders Co., 1953.

What
Turns
Women
On

Introduction: Turning On!

It is only in the last ten years or so that ordinary men and women have begun to be aware that they have a sexual personality which, while being a component of their complete personality as human beings, is as important in deciding how we behave and how we shape our lives as is the complete personality. In fact, the more we study human sexuality, the more it becomes apparent that the sexual side of our nature impinges on, and in many respects regulates and controls, the total sort of person we become.

When I was a boy, about half a century ago, sex was shrouded in secrecy. It was believed that men had certain sexual urges which now and again prompted, or even demanded, that they engage in sexual activities. We thought that these urges were more or less the same for everyone and that everyone reacted to them in more or less the same way. Of course we were aware that there were some men—not very many—who seemed to be obsessed with sex, if their goings-on were anything to go by, and we regarded them as mentally sick, unable to keep their sex-urges under decent control. The very occasional woman who behaved in a similar sexually abandoned way we looked upon with disgust, because women were not supposed to have sexual instincts, or if they had, were decent enough to smother them.

As a youngish teenager, I had an inkling that sex was not quite so grey as it was made out to be. I had discovered masturbation when I was between seven or eight years old; and between my initial experience and the arrival of full puberty at the age of twelve, which was early for those days, I used to masturbate two or three times a week. Not long after the onset of puberty, however, my sex-urges gradually began to increase the need to twice daily, and by the time I was fifteen and a half, to four daily outlets.

Realizing that this put me in the "sick, obsessed with sex" group, I tried to ignore these urges. I took all the old remedies—cold baths, exercise, sleeping with the bedroom windows wide open all the year through—and I pleaded with God to make me well, but all to no avail. Only by a superhuman effort was I very occasionally able to mesmerize the raging tensions in loins, belly, and cock. It was better than utter failure, but not enough to dispel the worry which constantly nagged me.

I had no one to go to for help or advice. This was the private and secret sector of my life, and one just didn't discuss it with anyone else. But I was intelligent enough to appreciate that if all my determined, deliberate efforts to keep my sex-urges under control failed, it was not my mind that was at fault. Maybe I was sick in my body, yet that was hard to believe, because I was, by sixteen and a half, a strapping youth of six feet, weighing 161 pounds, and with a physical endurance that made it possible to swim four or five miles, to walk thirty miles a day on the fells of the lake district, to enjoy a really hard day's fox hunting, with only a pleasant sensation of physical satiety at the end of it.

Fortunately, I have always been blessed (or cursed) with an inquiring mind. (My favorite reading then, as now, was encyclopedias of all kinds.) I decided that, if possible, I must find out what made me tick sexually, because I was sure that there was more to it than what one clasped in the hands.

There were not many books available in those days, but I did manage to procure copies of Krafft-Ebing's *Psychopathia Sexualis* and Havelock Ellis's *Studies in the Psychology of Sex* in a seedy Cambridge secondhand bookshop, and Freud's *Interpretation of Dreams* and *Totem and Tabu* in a shop in Charing Cross Road. Marie Stopes's *Married Love* was, of course, readily available, since at sixteen I had the bulk and a lot of the poise of a young man in his early twenties, and no one raised an eyebrow when I took it, together with that curious volume called *Aristotle's Works* (which the Greek philosopher certainly had no hand in concocting) from the shelves of a respectable bookshop in Colchester; and

3

I must have been one of the first to buy Van de Velde's *Ideal Marriage* and Malinowski's *The Sexual Life of Savages*.

When I had mastered his strange style, it was Van de Velde who gave me my first clear insight into the complexities of sex. But even he did not help me with my own problem, for though he referred to the effect of hormones on the sex-drive, he did not explicitly refer to the *degrees* of variation in sexual desire; he noted only two male types—"the potent" and "the weak."

By the time I had read Van de Velde I was seventeen, going on eighteen, and I had at least partially solved my particular worries. Pragmatic to a degree, I had argued that my frequent need for orgasm in order to relieve physical and psychic tensions was not harming me physically or psychologically. I had no difficulty in retaining my King's Scholarship; despite my almost complete failure to comprehend mathematics and all the sciences, I was either first, second, or third—never lower—in the fortnightly form orders; and I had acquired a School Certificate which exempted me from university matriculation. Though not a sportsman of the first class, I nevertheless had the stamina to achieve some prowess on and in the river, across country, and on the hockey field. After measles at fourteen, I was to have no other illness but the occasional bout of influenza until I parted company with two-thirds of my prostate at the age of fifty-four.

These measurable academic and sporting achievements and my, by now, quite considerable knowledge for a teenager, of sexual physiology and function, went a considerable way in helping me to accept my sexuality—though I did not then know what it was—but my greatest comfort I undoubtedly derived from the relationship I formed with a boy a year and a half my senior, whose sexual needs matched my own. We used to discuss our relative libidos and compare them with those of our acquaintances, whose sexual activities we knew to be far less frequent than our own. Though we did not understand what made us different, my friend always concluded any discussion we had with the sensible remark, "I don't care if I am different. All I know is that I find sex extremely pleasant, and I'm certain that nothing that is so pleasant can be bad for one." (We had not yet experienced alcohol.) I was more than inclined to agree with this comforting statement.

A little more than a year later, I was deeply engrossed in the Parisian experience to which I have referred briefly in *The Sensuous Couple*. Here I encountered sexual activities of such varying degrees of frequency and intensity as to leave no doubt in my mind that individual sexual needs differ across a very wide range. But my basic knowledge was still so imperfect that I was not tempted to analyze why this should be so. In any case, my practical involvement in sex left me in no mood nor with the time to give consideration to more "serious" and what one might almost term "academic" studies of the libido.

Naturally, my counseling left me in no doubt that

there was such a thing as sexual incompatibility, and that it sometimes played havoc with the marriage relationship. But even after World War II there was not yet widespread information about the influence of the sex hormones in regulating sexual desire, or even the knowledge that there did exist wide differences in individual sexual needs, leading to a tremendous variety of sexual behavior.

It was Kinsey's report on *Sexual Behavior in the Human Male* that first really brought the uncountable divergencies in sexual behavior to the general public. There was a great brouhaha which accompanied the publication of this report in 1948.

Within the confines of our own bed we were aware that we caressed one another's bodies, even the most initimate parts of them; but it shocked, and occasionally horrified us, to see the activities referred to, especially statistically, in cold print. Such passages as the following were almost too blatantly forceful to assimilate:

At upper social levels there may be considerable manual petting between partners, particularly on the part of the male who has been persuaded by the general talk among his companions, and by the codification of those opinions in the marriage manuals, that the female needs extended sensory stimulation if she is to be brought to simultaneous orgasm in coitus. Upper level petting involves the manual stimulation of all parts of the female body.

Manual manipulation of the female breast occurs regularly in 96 per cent of the histories of the married males of the upper level, and manual manipulation of the female genitalia is regularly found in about 90 per cent of the histories. The upper level believes that this petting is necessary for successful coital adjustment. . . .*

But if this required two or three readings for us to recover our composure sufficiently to take in the meaning, passages like this one really hit us between the eyes:

Under prolonged stimulation, as in heterosexual or group activities or in protracted homosexual activities, many a teen-age male will maintain a continuous erection for several hours, even when the physical contacts are at a minimum, and, in some cases, even after two or three ejaculations have occurred. . . .†

There were few who realized that such sexual stamina existed, and to be told that "many a teen-age male" was capable of it made many feel that the doctor and his associates were having some murky fun at our expense.

But it was the sections on frequency of what Kinsey sedately called "outlets," and the causes of the differences in frequency, which at last made it possible for people sexually constituted like myself to accept the fact that we were not freaks. By establishing the existence of differences in performance and capacity, the Kinsey report also laid the foundations upon which I and others similarly engaged in trying to help those who were sexually upset might base our studies of individual sexual behavior, in the

* Alfred C. Kinsey, *Sexual Behavior in the Human Male* (Philadelphia: W. B. Saunders Co., 1948), p. 367.
† Kinsey, *Sexual Behavior in the Human Male*, p. 231.

hope of helping more than we were helping at the moment.

By the late 1950s, I had become firmly convinced that by hook or by crook it must be got over to the layman that he had a sexual character as well as a general character. It so happened that I was prompted at this time to write a marriage manual in order to propagate certain ideas which I had formulated through my counseling.

By this time there was quite an array of marriage manuals available. All of them I regarded, perhaps arrogantly, to have a number of flaws. I proposed addressing mine exclusively to women—all the others were for couples—but I saw no reason why I should not eliminate from mine one of the chief flaws of the rest, namely, the pseudomedical terms and the often coy language in which they were written. I would employ the vernacular as far as I could without infringing taste. I would write "putting the penis in the vagina," instead of "penetration;" I would say "making love" instead of "copulation," "sexual intercourse" or "coitus;" I would talk about "sucking the penis" and "licking the clitoris" instead of "oral caresses." I wanted to use "coming" and "coming off" instead of "reaching orgasm" or "climaxing," but even the sixteenth publisher to whom I submitted it and who offered to publish it jibbed at that. (*Mainly for Wives* eventually appeared in 1962; and I smile now when I think of the sedate language of the book which the Marriage Guidance Council considered "scandalous," and the language I am able to use only eleven years later.)

My main objectives in *Mainly for Wives* were to suggest (i) that making love imposed equal responsibilities on both partners so that each provided the other with the most intense sensations at coming off, in other words, that the woman must be as active as the man during physical lovemaking; (ii) that by both doing this it was possible for each to show the other the depth of the emotional love they felt for one another, which could not be adequately expressed in any other way; and (iii)—the most revolutionary of all—that if the woman wanted to make love, but her partner was not too keen, there was no reason why she should not initiate lovemaking and be the *active* partner from first caress to climax.

To explain why this could happen, I made my first fumbling attempt to describe the differences in sexual character in terms a layman could understand. (I believe I am the first to have done so.) I wrote:

> The sexual urge is as valid a characteristic of a man or a woman as are fair hair and beautiful large brown eyes, or even temper and a quick wit. It is an essential component of a person's total make-up, and can no more be ignored or changed than can any other physical or psychological characteristic.
>
> The sexual character falls into three main types, which apply equally to men and women, and are classified thus: the highly-sexed (or passionate), the medium-sexed, and the lowly-sexed. These classifications are roughly based on the frequency of the sexual urge. The medium-sexed, who form by far the largest group of men and women, and can therefore be said

to represent the norm, experience sexual desire, arousal and the need for orgasm two or three times a week (in their twenties an average of four times); the lowly-sexed may experience sexual desire, arousal and the need for orgasm only once a fortnight, or once a month; while the highly-sexed have a daily urge, and often a twice- or thrice-daily urge.

To the medium-sexed and the lowly-sexed, it may come as a surprise to find that there are men and women who have such a frequent urge as this last. I think all of us have had sufficient experience to realise that there are people whose interest in sex appears to be one of their predominant features. I have a shrewd suspicion, too, that we rather disapprove of such people. We are inclined to interpret their high sexuality as being an unhealthy interest in sex which they make no attempt to control, but, on the contrary, stimulate and encourage their desire for sexual activity, the means for achieving which they seem to go out of their way to discover. In other words, they make no attempt at self-control.

In much the same way, and this is particularly true of men, we are apt to despise the lowly-sexed. Their apparent disinterest in sex seems to us to display a lack of manhood and womanhood, making of them creatures belonging almost to a sub-species.

We are wrong to condemn either the highly-sexed or the lowly-sexed, and if we do think like this, it shows very clearly that we are quite ignorant of the nature of the sexual urge, and the varying degrees of sexuality which different people possess.

(Since I wrote these words in 1959, I have been caught up in the sexual revolution which has taken place over the last dozen years or so. I have become more involved in research, and am proud to think that I may have made useful contributions to our understanding of sexuality. In the course of this, I have revised a number of my views on and attitudes toward a number of aspects of sexual behavior. Certainly as a result of research into the sex-drive, I have modified some of the statements in the passages from *Mainly for Wives* which I have just quoted. I shall be referring to these presently.)

It was the publication of Masters and Johnson's *Human Sexual Response* in 1966 that was the most outstanding milestone in our understanding of sexuality. No one had previously made scientific observations of sexual activity; and though many of Masters and Johnson's findings, e.g., the "sex-flush reaction," can be of little interest to the layman, their conclusions as a whole have revealed many of the ramifications of sexuality not before known to exist, which enable people like myself to have a deeper understanding of sexuality, which we can pass on to those who come to us for help and to the wider audience who read our books.

The next milestone in our understanding of sexuality was without doubt the publication in 1967 of *Forum: The Journal of Human Relations*, with which I am proud to have been associated throughout its existence, except for the first few months, during which we were discovering one another. Published monthly by Penthouse International, *Forum*, more than either Kinsey or Masters and Johnson, has been instrumental in bringing the existence of sexuality in all its shades to the consciousness of the layman. By making available the experiences of men and women of all degrees of sexuality and every possible concept of sexual behavior to a wide public, its greatest achievement, in my view, has been the reassurance it has given to people who were previously made unhappy by the private fear that they were sexually kinky or in some way sexually inadequate.

By printing the "confessions" of men and women who had off-beat sexual preferences, *Forum* quelled the fears of those puzzled by their own sexual needs. It was a policy that in the early days brought down opprobrium on the heads of editors and contributors alike. We were convinced, however, that though the magazine might be used as an aid to masturbation—and what was wrong with that?—our serious treatment of all aspects of sexuality must, in the end, bear fruit. And so it has turned out. For more than five years the magazine has been attacked as a mercenary exploitation of pornography by the national press, Mrs. Mary Whitehouse and Lord Longford, who wrote in his (unofficial) report *Pornography:*

> However sincerely conceived as a beneficial service to those with problems or inadequate sexual knowledge, *Forum* cannot avoid appealing also—we would suggest largely—to those whose interest is salacious, prurient, or fantasist. This must stimulate precisely the furtive obsessions which the magazine purports to relieve by open discussion. (p. 309)

Now, however, the "heavies," as we call them, are beginning to be approving and complimentary. Doctors, too, are finding us useful. The psychiatric establishments have always been sympathetic and are now beginning to be forthright in their approval of us. There is evidence that though we have not deliberately set out to change our image—except in one or two small details—we have nevertheless ceased to become the masturbatory adjunct we once were. Laymen (and professionals) read us because they know that they will invariably learn something new about human sexuality from any number of *Forum* that happens to come their way. They have confidence in us, also, because our contributors and advisers are acknowledged experts in their fields.

Personally, I believe—and would so believe had I never had any contact with the magazine except as a reader—that *Forum*, in Europe at all events, has been the chief influence in the sexual lives of hundreds of thousands of men and women, and has created more sexual happiness than any other single agency in the field of sexual enlightenment. By holding up ordinary men and women as mirrors for other ordinary men and women to see themselves in, by applying the discoveries of the experts to the needs of ordinary men and women in terms they can easily understand, and, above all, by displaying sincere sympathy for everyone with problems and encouragement for the happy as well as the unhappy, the journal has brought to a considerable portion of humanity the recognition that they are sexual beings and not just fucking machines. By so doing, it has brought about a broadening of the human personality, not among the ranks of those of already outstanding talent, but among

13

Mr. Everyman and Mrs. Everywoman. I only hope that eventually, when it has overcome its opposition from the American Lord Longfords, Mary Whitehouses, and Malcolm Muggeridges, it will have the same beneficent effect on the lives of ordinary American men and women.

If I have made it sound that by one good cause or another a miracle has overtaken the sexual understanding of very many men and women, all right, so it has! But I hasten to add that so far, only the very fringe of the shroud in which sex has been enveloped over the centuries has been lifted. Even the experts readily admit that there is much still which is not understood. This is certainly true of human sexual response (or sexuality) and more particularly of the sexual response of women.

There is no doubt about it, but Women's Lib certainly has a point when it claims that the majority of women have, up to now, been second-class citizens sexually. Despite the fact that I came along ten years ago with *Mainly for Wives* and urged women not to be sexually passive all the time—I get very fed up sometimes when I get abusive letters calling me a "male chauvinist pig" since I am actually the founder of Sexual Women's Lib—comparatively few average-sexed women have taken my advice. (The highly-sexed woman has *always* done her own sex thing.)

In this male-sex-dominated world we have put the emphasis more on male sexuality than on female sexuality. When we have considered female sexuality at all, it has always been vis-à-vis the male's sexual role, and we have interpreted the male sexual role from the point of view of the male's experience of sex. In fact, by regarding the male as the sexual initiator we have actually been saying that without men there cannot be any sex.

To a certain extent this is true. If the man can't get a hard-on, there can't be any fucking. Whereas the penis can enter the vagina when the woman is not sexually roused, unless the man is roused the penis can't get in. More than that, however, we have also placed men's sexual needs first. It has been his sexual tensions that have regulated the frequency of a couple's intercourse; delicate sexual creature that he is—and this is in large part true—it has been the woman who has been warned not to do or say anything that might make him feel sexually inadequate, because feelings of sexual inadequacy are the main cause of his failure to function sexually as he ought to. Make disparaging remarks about the size of his penis and he won't get an erection; on the other hand, show too much eagerness and he'll come too soon.

The sexual dice have always been loaded against the woman. If she doesn't climax easily, thereby suggesting that her partner lacks expertise as a lover, his sexual self-esteem will take a knock. By hook or by crook, she has got to be made to respond, whether she is feeling like it or not. Should she try to convince him that she can be perfectly happy by making her body available for his satisfaction, he will not believe her. If she feels sexually inadequate, it is she who is responsible, not he.

It is true, however, that there is a difference between male and female sexual response. The average man who has no psychological or functional problem is more quickly roused and more easily brought to climax than the average woman. Give him a vagina and an erection and he simply cannot fail to ejaculate and experience orgasm with resulting relief from tension. On the other hand, give a woman an erect penis and it is by no means certain that she will climax unless she gets a good deal of help from her partner. However, it is more than possible that the traditionally slower response of women is precisely that. Traditional. A great deal of human reaction, especially in the gut area of sexuality, is culturally conditioned.

This difference in physical response has been at the bottom of the classification of women as inferior sexual creatures. The idea of inferiority has deprived women of a sexuality worthy of consideration, and the emphasis in the study of sexuality has been on the male and his sex-drive and his sexual responses and behavior.

The average-sexed male is, in fact, a sexually sensitive being. At the height of his sexual maturity, between twenty-five and thirty-five, he has a double arousal system, the cerebral and the tactile, each of which is equally efficient at producing erection and its accompanying sexual desire. If he looks at pictures of sexually desirable women, or fantasizes that he is involved in a sexually exciting situation, his brain sends messages via his spinal column to his erection center near the base of the spine, and his penis springs to attention forthwith, and his genital system throbs with tension that will only be relieved by ejaculation and orgasm. To demonstrate what a potent sexual stimulator his brain is, there are a number of young men who are able to make themselves come off purely by fantasizing sexually, without any tactile stimulation of the penis. The reverse is equally true. A few seconds manual or oral stimulation of the penis sends messages to the brain, which shoots them back spontaneously to the erection center and at once induces erection and tension. The tension then invades the brain with sexual thoughts and desires.

Because of this cerebral connection with the physical sexual system, the male has a whole range of stimulators with which to arouse himself sexually. The suggestion of a sexually attractive female body covered by clothes, the sight of a naked female body which is sexually attractive to him, pictures and statues of desirable women, sounds which have sexual connotations, the sight of sexual activities, written and spoken accounts of sexual activities and situations, and discussing sexual matters are all unfailing stimulants to the majority of average-sexed men.

Equally unfailing are his responses to tactile stimulation. If he begins foreplay with the softest of soft penises, within seconds of a caress on any of his erogenous zones the limp, even timid, organ is stiffly upstanding, arrogant and aggressive. If he begins foreplay exhibiting no signs of sexual arousal, as soon as he begins to caress his partner sexually, though she may make not the faintest move toward him, he is physically prepared for every sexual eventuality.

There are few average-sexed women who respond with a comparative immediacy. It takes some minutes of actual tactile stimulation, even of a woman's chief sensitive zone, her clitoris, before that organ erects, and her sex-glands begin to produce signs of excitement in the form of lubricating fluids. On their own admission, women are rarely sexually stirred immediately by pictorial representations of sex. Though they have a cerebral arousal system, the signs are that it operates at a much slower speed than the male's. In fact, many males believe that it does not really exist.

While not denying women some kind of sexuality, it has become a widespread male belief that it would be ill-spent time to try to discover what it is all about. When I was discussing it with an experienced young man the other day, he said, "What sort of sexuality can it be that lets a woman let a man fuck her and not want to come because it may require more effort than she is prepared to make? Or what sort of sexuality is it that doesn't turn a woman on when she watches a blue film? Ever heard of a woman with a fetish? All right, so only a small percentage of men are fetishists, but you'd think there would be a few women? More than 99 percent of men masturbate from adolescence; but Kinsey says that the peak of female masturbation occurs in the forties age-group, and then the maximum percentage is only sixty."

In fact, if he had had the book handy, he could have quoted from *Sexual Behavior in the Human Female* (p. 520) the following table relating to the number of orgasms which the average female and male had ever had before marriage:

Activity to orgasm	Accumulative incidence		Average (mean) number of orgasms	
	Female	*Male*	*Female*	*Male*
Total Outlet	64%	100%	223	1523
Masturbation	41%	94%	130	872
Nocturnal Dreams	12%	82%	6	175
Petting	37%	26%	37	64
Coitus	27%	80%	39	330
Homosexual	5%	30%	11	75
Animal Contacts	—	8%	—	7

"And isn't it a sign of superior sexuality," my young man might have asked, "that there are very few men who don't fantasize frequently either when they are masturbating or fucking, and yet who has heard of a woman fantasizing?"

The truth of the matter is that women have been more reticent about displaying their sexuality than men. After all, when you've a limb that enlarges and stiffens and becomes a throbbing presence the moment you have a sexual thought—and often when you haven't consciously had a sexual thought—how can you not know that you are a sexual creature? Isn't it natural that because the woman's equipment cannot be seen by herself or by her partner unless it is scrupulously looked for, that she should be more modest in her own evaluation of her sexuality?

19

You've got to take notice of an erect penis; you're lucky if you can catch a glimpse of erect clitoris!

It is this arrogant male self-assessment of his sexual role as hunter and his bludgeoning persuasion of the female that she is the victim, that has been responsible for the woman concealing her sexuality, even from herself. Recall the time, still within living memory, when "nice" women did not have orgasms. Just before I wrote *Mainly for Wives,* I was discussing the woman's sex-role with an octogenarian woman friend.

"I loved my husband," she told me, "worshipped the ground he walked on, and until he died—he was sixty-two—he made frequent love to me, as you would say. Yes, I had some sensations, but only once or twice so strongly that they seemed to overwhelm me. I was a young girl then, and I was very frightened, and was always on my guard that they should not happen. An acquaintance of mine, who had the reputation of being very fast, once asked me if I ever had such experiences and didn't I think they were the most wonderful thing that could happen. I was horrified, and denied that they had ever happened to me, and I told her that if she wished to remain on friendly terms with me she would never talk about such things to me again."

Even when Marie Stopes rediscovered the orgasm for women in the 1920s, she did not improve matters. In fact, she made them worse. When she told women that if their partners did not bring them off every time they made love, they (the partners) were unworthy to be considered lovers, but did not tell them what they must do to help themselves reach orgasm, she did nothing to change the sexually passive role of woman, and, indeed, encouraged men to be even more aggressive. If women demanded orgasm, but did not respond readily and were not willing to be active participants, then, damn it, they would have to put up with what was coming to them.

Ten years ago, the doctor who wrote the foreword to the English edition of *Mainly for Wives* wrote this:

> . . . . the fear of practical sex that is encountered in clinics where young wives attend for advice and help because they are childless cannot be appreciated unless one has first-hand experience of it. Many of these young women have never enjoyed normal intercourse, some, no form of intercourse at all. Until they have plucked up the courage to visit the clinic to seek advice, they have tolerated this situation because either they have had no sex instruction in early years or the sex instruction they were given was faulty; or other women have told them that 'sex' is just something for men.

Well, things are not quite so bad as that nowadays, but the improvement has not been all that great. While there has been a drive to persuade women that they are sexual beings, little has been done to reveal their sexuality to themselves, or to their partners. I have been as remiss as anyone in this respect.

To be honest, I have tended to regard women as sexual creatures all my life. Looking back on what

21

I have written in books and in *Forum* articles, and in other forms of teaching, this flaw stares me in the face and assails me with self-recrimination. You have only to glance through *The Sensuous Couple* to see from my exhortations to the would-be sensuous woman, exactly how I have taken for granted the equality of women's sexuality with men's.

Perhaps the fault is founded on the fact that from my first heterosexual experience when I was thirteen, which happily was fantastically successful, the half-dozen or so women I have made love to have all had sexual personalities of their own that certainly matched mine. Perhaps thirty-two years of marriage to such a woman, despite my forty years of trying to help hundreds of sexually unhappy women, made me unperceptive to the more widespread true situation.

My good friend Nancy Friday first hit me right between the eyes with what the true situation is when she was gathering material for her book, *My Secret Garden: Women's Sexual Fantasies*,* and we discussed some of the amazing confessions which women had made to her. Of course I was aware that some women fantasized, because a few had confided in me. But without exception, my fantasizing women had problems, and they fantasized to try to overcome them. That women should come near to equaling men in the frequency of their fantasizing, and often excel them in the content of their fantasies was a revelation. Even Kinsey had not

* Nancy Friday, *My Secret Garden: Women's Sexual Fantasies* (New York: Trident Press, 1973).

hinted at this. In fact, while allowing that women do fantasize, he commented:

> But most males in our sample (84 per cent) indicated that they were at least sometimes, and in most instances often aroused by thinking of sexual relations with females. . . . Such erotic stimulation probably occurs more often than any other type of psychologic stimulation among males.
>
> A smaller percentage (69 per cent) of the females in the sample reported that they had ever had erotic fantasies about males, and nearly a third (31 per cent) insisted that they had never been aroused by thinking about males or of sexual relations with them.*

While Miss Friday was assessing her material, I was busy with a survey of my own on the "sex-drive." Working with 370 couples who were either married or had a regular relationship going, from their recorded sexual activities over a period of four weeks I arrived at two main conclusions. First, that the majority of couples make love more often in response to what I called their "voluntary" sex-drive than to their "involuntary" sex-drive. (The "involuntary" sex-drive operates when we respond to the chemical reactions which take place in our bodies, and over which we have no control. This happens to the average, healthy man, who engages in no sexual activity except in response to his chemical reactions, roughly every three and a half days. In women it appears to be less regular and less frequent, but many will recognize what I mean by

---

* Kinsey, *Sexual Behavior in the Human Female* (Philadelphia: Saunders, 1953), p. 665.

the spontaneous arousal they experience just before menstruation begins, and in the three or four days after the period has finished. But we do not have to wait for the "involuntary" sex-drive to operate in order to be roused sexually. Both men and women are capable of being roused at will by either tactile or psychologic stimuli. This type of arousal-at-will I term the "voluntary" sex-drive.) Second, that women who recognize that they have sexual personalities of their own, are as sexually imaginative as men and as sexually responsive; that they are, in fact, as fully equipped to be active partners as men are.*

A good deal of the evidence tended to show that given the wish and the encouragement women in all walks of life and all age-groups, who have uninhibited, sexually imaginative, and technically expert partners, are as appreciative of lovemaking as men are; many can, in fact, develop their sexuality independent of their partners and can draw out the partner in ways that formerly we believed were applicable only to men.

Let me briefly reiterate what has been widely held to be the differences between male sexual response and female sexual response. Men, we have been told, have a more highly developed sexuality because they have a double arousal system—cerebral and tactile, or in other terms, psychological and physiological—both of which produce responses at high speed. Women also have a double arousal sys-

---

* Robert Chartham, *Your Sex-Drive: Myths, Manias and Mastery* (New York: Pinnacle Books, 1973).

tem, but their physiological system is superior to their psychological system, and even their physiological system produces responses at a much slower rate than the man's.

Thus, a man achieves almost instantaneous erection by thinking about desirable female bodies, looking at photographs and statues of desirable female bodies, observing actual desirable female bodies clothed or unclothed, fantasizing about past sexual activities or imagining sexual activities, reading erotic literature, listening to erotic recitals and sounds, anticipating the results of sexual activity and by sexually caressing the partner. These are his psychological stimuli. He also responds to caresses by his partner of any of his sensitive zones, especially his penis and scrotum, to chance bodily contacts even when his mind is empty of sexual thoughts, to other tactile agencies such as fur, smooth materials like silk and velvet, to flowing water, if he is entirely naked, to vibrations from machines, and so on. These and more are acknowledged to be his physiological stimuli.

By contrast, a woman, we have been told, is very badly off. On her own, she is rarely roused by thoughts of sexual activities even with her husband or boyfriend. She does not respond to thoughts of desirable male bodies, nor to photographs and statues of male nudes. She seldom responds to the sight of the actual male nude body, though she may if there is an erection present. She does not respond easily, if at all, to fantasizing about past sexual activities. She does respond fairly frequently to erotic literature and to discussions of sexual matters. She responds to a certain degree to caressing her partner's body, especially to fondling a limp penis into erection, and often just watching an erection developing is enough to make her respond. Once she is roused, however, she can respond to many of these psychological stimuli, thus enhancing the total experience. But she relies chiefly for arousal on the caresses of her partner, and is, therefore, much more dependent than him on physiological rather than psychological stimuli for her initial arousal.

But is this really so? It was the remarks of a number of my women sex-drive collaborators that made me begin to wonder, and I decided that it would be worthwhile investigating. So I wrote to a number of women who had previously consulted me, picking their names at random, and I made an appeal in the British and American editions of *Forum* to women, asking any who would collaborate to supply me with answers to the questions which follow.

The questions I asked were: Are you sexually roused by—

(a) a man's physical appearance. If so, describe your "sexy" male.

(b) other male qualities, if appearance does NOT turn you on, or only partially turns you on.

(c) pictures, photographs, statues. If so, describe them and the object that turns you on most.

(d) books and so on, i.e., the written word. If so, describe them and identify your favorite book or passage.

(e) pornography of any kind, e.g., written, photographic, drawings, blue films, "live" shows, etc.

(f) erotic thoughts or fantasies. Describe them.

(g) music. If so, which kind? Name any particular piece or pieces.

(h) discussing sexual matters. If so, what?

(i) sadistic acts.

(j) masochistic acts.

(k) fetishes.

(l) the brush or feel of certain objects, e.g., silk, velvet, fur, smooth stones, flowing water, any other object.

(m) sight of a naked partner (i) without erection (ii) with erection.

(n) caressing the partner, especially his penis.

(o) one particular caress by the partner. If so, describe.

(p) anything else not mentioned above.

These questions fall into six main classifications:

    I. Visual (questions a, b, c and m)

    II. Psychological (questions d, f, g and h)

    III. Touch (questions k, l, n and o)

    IV. Pornography (question e)

    V. Sadomasochism (questions i and j)

    VI. Individual responses (question p)

One hundred ninety-eight women replied—119 American, 79 British; 73 from my files, 125 from *Forum*. Their answers were the most detailed of any returned in the various other surveys I have made. The youngest was sixteen and the oldest forty-six. There were one or two who betrayed a responsiveness above the average, but most were "girls next door" who will admit to being sexual creatures, and admit, too, that they enjoy being sexual creatures.

Under the six headings I noted above, let them tell you themselves how they respond to sex, and let us see what comes out.

1

In the Eye of the Beholder

THE VISUAL STIMULI to which all men and women respond sexually are in essence psychological stimuli. We see something to which the brain immediately attaches a sexual significance, the brain flashes messages down our spinal column to our sexual arousal mechanism, and hey presto! we are turned on.

As I pointed out in the last chapter, men respond immediately to a great variety of such visual stimuli. One of the chief is the female body, nude or suggestively draped, and sexually desirable to the beholder. The spontaneous reaction is, "I wouldn't mind laying her!" and great pal that he is, up comes the penis in helpful erection, at the ready should circumstances permit thought to be transformed into deed.

But we each have our ideals of physical sexual beauty, which is just as well since not all women are cast in the same mold. Some men, for example, go for huge breasts; others, of whom I am one, are turned off by monstrous boobs and are roused only by those perfectly proportioned to the rest of the body.

Many men do not "specialize" in one part of the female anatomy, but make their ideal a combination of certain features: for example, long, shapely legs with a small bosom and longish black hair and pale blue eyes; or a Scandinavian blonde with full, moist lips and a tight almost buttockless bottom; or brown hair, a large bosom, and a prominent bottom that wriggles excitingly with each step she takes; or a long neck, dark hair, deep brown eyes, a bust little bigger than a boy's, narrow hips, small bottom, and slender thighs; or a girl who is big and plump all over.

Some men cannot tell you what features or combination of features turn them on. They have no doubt that the attraction is physical, however, and that it is an overall impression which communicates itself to them. One often hears the word "sulky" used in such cases, or "hot," or "fiery," or even "cold." Whatever the word is, it is not intended to convey an attitude of mind but an attitude of body.

Each of us has our interpretation of such descriptions. For me, "sulky" conveys the impression that the girl will be expert in the techniques of love-making, that she will build up her responses and mine in a slow crescendo of little climaxes over a long period of uninhibited mutual caressing, that the grand climax, when allowed to arrive, will be produced by long, slow but deliberate thrusts of pelvis and counterthrusts of buttocks, taking minutes to develop and then bursting over the lovers simultaneously in a cloud of utter voluptuousness. "Hot," on the other hand, expresses for me the girl who is easily roused, is frankly physical in her demands of sex, who lets her partner know the quality of her responses, has no time for sultry dalliance because she can climax time and time again, and who during coupling will probably be more active than her mate. "Fiery" differs from "hot" in my vocabulary by implying a session of threshing limbs, nips, bites, really demanding fellatio, a display of more activity than she wants from her partner—the leader in programming—which will nevertheless be extempore, constant vocalization, and a shrill climax. To others each of these terms may mean something different from my own expectations.

My definitions, while they are all physically related, make me respond psychologically, and this, according to Kinsey, is the main difference in sexual response between men and women. Kinsey goes so far as to attribute the woman's failure to climax during coupling to the ease with which she is distracted, and the man's almost nonexistent failure rate to his being less easy to distract because his responses are psychological in origin. Kinsey's actual words are:

The slower responses of the female in coitus appear to depend in part upon the fact that she frequently does not begin to respond as promptly as the male, because psychologic stimuli usually play a more important role in the arousal of the average male, and a less important role in the sexual arousal of the average female. The average male is aroused in anticipation of a sexual relationship, and he usually comes to erection and is ready to proceed directly to orgasm as soon as or even before he makes any actual contact. The average female, on the contrary, is less often aroused by such anticipation, and sometimes she does not begin to respond until there has been a considerable amount of physical stimulation.

Moreover, because she is less aroused by psychologic stimuli, the female is more easily distracted than the male in the course of her coital relationships. The male may be continuously stimulated by seeing the female, by engaging in erotic conversation with her, by thinking of the sexual techniques he may use, by remembering some previous sexual experience, by planning later contacts with the same female or some other sexual partner, and by any number of other psychologic stimuli which keep him aroused even though he may interrupt his coital contacts. Perhaps two-thirds of the females find little if any arousal in such psychologic stimuli. Consequently, when the steady build-up of the female's response is interrupted by the male's cessation of movement, changes of position, conversation, or temporary withdrawal from genital union, she drops back to or toward a normal physiologic state from which she has to start again when the physical contacts are renewed. . . .*

At another point Kinsey says that many women are easily distracted during loveplay and actual coupling by a door banging, the return of children, the telephone ringing, a knock at the door or ring of a doorbell, imagined threats of interruption, but

---

* Kinsey, *Sexual Behavior in the Human Female*, pp. 626–7.

that men rarely are and only by a direct threat of intervention. He also notes the same lack of psychological concentration in the females of some animal species, e.g., female cats and dogs will eat during copulation, but males will not, female cats will also watch mouseholes and actually attempt to chase mice while mounted, but males will not.

In view of this, one would not expect many women to have anything approaching the same interest in the male body as the male has in the female body. But let's see what some of them say.

A Man's Physical Appearance

Of my 198 correspondents, 153 (more than two-thirds) claim to have their physically ideal male, who is ideal because his appearance or some feature actually rouses them sexually. As you will see, they are as definite in their likes and dislikes as most men are in this respect.

Margy is sixteen and still at school. She lives in London, England.

"I hope I'm not considered 'too young' to be of any use in your research. I've been fucking since I was thirteen, so I do have a good idea about what turns me on.

"*Physical appearance*. What I really love is a guy with *long legs*. Not very muscular ones, but slightly 'meaty' ones. There is nothing worse than a man with skinny legs. I don't like the 'no-arsed-wonders' that seem to be so popular with my friends. I like a backside that you can actually see and really feel.

"Pink, juicy-looking nipples really make my clit throb. I can't stand men with nasty little brown nipples.

"If the man has very dark hair, then lots of it all over his body is very rousing. But I think what makes me moist quicker than anything is a young, teenage, 'feminine' blond, hairless guy. I like skin to be pale, but not pasty. Deep tans do nothing for me at all.

"I find that with older men (early forties) I'd rather not see their bodies. I'm generalising a bit because I've only seen about half a dozen, but what I've seen have been slightly on the middle-aged-spread side. A young body definitely turns me on more and quicker."

There is a clue to Margy's preference for young teenage "feminine" boys in another answer, where she admits to having lesbian fantasies.

Kate is twenty-two, married, and lives in Britain.

"Yes, I am turned on by a man's physical appearance. My 'sexy' male is tall, good-looking, twenty to thirty. He must wear trendy clothes, especially those lovely tight trousers, to show off a nice round bottom. I saw a superb specimen waiting at my bus stop the other day, and his bottom was so gorgeous, I decided I just had to take a later bus, and go to the nearest loo and work myself off. It was fantastic. My husband has a lovely bottom, too. I often wish I had a cock so that I could go up it. But it isn't so beautiful as that boy's. I couldn't get it out of my mind. When we had it off that night, I stroked my husband's bottom imagining it was the bus-stop boy's. It was a cloudburst, when I came."

Elizabeth lives in England in one of the great provincial towns of the west country.

"These are my answers," she began, "in order of association. (In trying to formulate them, I came to the conclusion that although I have a vivid imagination, in most ways my sexual imagination seems pretty dry—probably due to a very repressive upbringing.) By the way, I am twenty-seven and single and heterosexual.

"I am sexually aroused by—

"Certainly by a man's appearance. The theory that women don't share the impersonal, masculine (so called) roving eye is a load of codswallop. I enjoy looking at men when I walk down the street, especially their hip action. One game I often play to pass the time in trains or buses is to look around at all the males and choose which one I would go to bed with, if I had to go to bed with any one of them. Sometimes I think I couldn't make it with any of them even at knife point (when they're a seedy-looking lot) and once I got into a compartment in the tube (subway) with three men who were all so sexy I couldn't make up my mind between them. I became so absorbed that I went right past my station and didn't come to until I reached Brixton.

"My idea of a sexy male is someone with a good figure (not flabby or like wet string), broad shoulders, narrow hips, and delicate facial features—someone with a twinkle in his eye and a look of fitness and energy—thick curly hair and full lips, also nice teeth and healthy gums. Missing teeth give me the creeps, so do falsies and baldness. I like firm muscles and a look of solidity about a man, and also a look of mischief or playfulness. Albert Finney is one of my ideals. So is Omar Sharif, but he's a bit solemn. Academic-looking types don't seem sexy to me. I like a certain athleticism, but not wrestlers or boxers. Anthony Quinn is not bad. As far as bodies go, the *Javelin Thrower* in Delphi museum is my idea of a super body and Rodin's *The Kiss* is very arousing.

"However, it's hard to separate the mental and physical, and in spite of ideal standards, there are probably not many men, however ugly, who wouldn't appeal to me ultimately if there was a strong mental link and they were good lovers. Often good-looking men turn out to be a lot less sensual and proficient than their more imperfect counterparts.

"Back to looks—certain races appeal more than others. There's nothing like the Irish—the most lyrical lovers of all. Italians *look* good, so do the French and many Indians. Anglo-Saxons don't look very sexy, but often are.

"Personally, I don't idolise tall men, although I like to feel I've got something of pleasing substantiality in my arms, otherwise I feel like a mother putting my arms round a child instead of a lover.

"Physical fitness and good posture are important to me, also a healthy look. A lot of English men (and women) don't take care of their bodies.

"Beards and long hair have a mental appeal, but

I don't like a lot of hair on the chest as it seems ape-like and you can't feel the warm skin so well through it. I like smooth, supple skin that is not rough to touch.

"Bodies mean more to me than faces. Straight features have an aesthetic but not a sexual appeal. It is the movement of the body and set of the bones which gives that aura of sex and masculinity.

"What more? Oh, yes—men's backs naked over a pair of jeans are one of the most arousing sights this world has to offer."

I cannot imagine what Elizabeth might have written if her sexual imagination had equaled in vividness the rest of her imagination, and she had had a sexually liberated upbringing instead of "a very repressive" one! However, to be serious, she seems to have taken good measure of the nature of her sexuality and doesn't hesitate to give it free rein.

Anita lives in Sacramento, California. She is twenty-three, college-educated, majored in drama, with strong emphasis on psychology, sociology, and political science. She is radical in politics and "quite interested in alternate living styles—and definitely countercultural."

"I am very definitely turned on by physical appearances—any attractive man on the street. Am particularly turned on by short, slender graceful types with (very important) nice hands, eyes, and small features, preferably 'cute.' The three guys that I have been turned on by were of this type. I am, by the way, of average height, five feet six, average weight, 108 pounds, measurements average, 34, 23, 33—not a big person. Part of my preference is due to the fact that I honestly can't stand guys bigger than myself and, in fact, am *grossed* out by big clumsy-looking people—women included. Also, my father is small and there is a bisexual leaning in my tastes. Small men often seem to have lively, bright personalities to maybe compensate for size. Sure they turn me on, though.

"My present lover is relatively interesting and I'm highly attracted to him. He is five feet seven, small-boned, 130 pounds, with the slight but athletic body of a dancer, broad shoulders, slender hips, though not as small as mine, muscular, and has a cat-like grace and agility. Hands the same size as mine, slender neck, small feet, small straight features, basically a highly masculine face—thick black eyebrows, heavy forehead, very angular face-shape, wide full mouth (I like wide mouths), big heavily lashed eyes, very thick but always clean-shaven beard, heavy moustache and sideburns (all of which I dig very much). He has to shave twice a day, that heavy five o'clock shadow really turns me on. Arms a little on the hairy side, so is chest some. Rather nice. The combination of almost extreme masculinity on a very finely boned and featured man are fantastic."

Elsewhere Anita gives a possible clue to her liking for small men, though she suspects, "I am rather normal, slightly liberal, with a slightly kinky taste for little guys." She goes on, "I have had trouble with sex, particularly early. Men started reacting very obviously and strongly long before I knew how to cope with it. Relatives particularly bad. Made me a bit reticent for a while, but growing up has helped that. Now my sex gives me a sense of power and though I rarely use it like this, I definitely like it."

She also believes she may have a "fairly high male hormone supply. Pubic hair very thick, with somewhat of a male growth pattern, heavy secondary hair, particularly (much more than most men before plucking) eyebrows, also light periods, a tendency towards muscles, shoulders a little wide, with hips distinctly a bit narrower, also a tendency to a male-like pattern of weight gain and loss."

Though she has a number of inhibitions still, she is approaching the highly-sexed. "If lover was around would like to make love at least one or two times a day, if he's not around I masturbate every one and a half days or get very irritable. Have fainted from the sensations got from masturbating. Hope to do it soon making love with him. Inclined to be very quiet when coming and very little movement—part habit, I'd hate to be overheard. Inclined very definitely to try to get closer. Very much inclined towards monogamy, partially because I probably wouldn't get much out of a casual lay in the way of good technique. If I don't get anything out of it, I'm not going to ball—period. Lover and I talk about menstruation and everything. If he acted 'funny' about periods, or balling during periods, I'd ditch him. With good reason. Men with hang-ups I don't want."

Anita is, in fact, something of a puzzle. I shall be returning to other parts of her letter later.

Iris lives in Toronto, Canada. She is twenty-three and has been a prostitute for three and a half years. She says, "I have always been turned on by a man's physical appearance, but when I was younger I was only aroused by men in clothing, men who knew how to dress and accent their best features. Most of my affairs—not my clients—were blonde, tall and lean, but they were always sharp dressers. It was a turn on to be seen with them in public. Up until my current affair, and the one just previous to it, most of my men would not be labelled movie stars as types, but they were memorable because they were unique looking and had style.

"Suddenly, about two and a half years ago, I changed. A year before that I was a dancer and on a gig I met a black musician who was breaking into The Game. I thought I loved him, but I only went on the streets for him, because he was cool and classy, and every black chick in Toronto knew him. He was a fantastically talented drummer for an up and coming group, and when I walked into the club after work, everyone knew I was his woman.

"He was approximately six foot two and slender. He sported a beautiful afro and a deep scar in his right cheek. His features were white more than black, and I suppose it was likely because he was a mulatto. Naked he seemed almost too slim, but he had a cool grace that I found irresistible.

"Right after I left my tall, dark pimp, I met Pat who was handsome, dark-haired, and blue-eyed.

Pat was very popular, in fact he had six girls, but after I finally got him to myself, I didn't want him. Then I met Bill, my present lover. He was a bartender and we grew to be friends. I thought he was handsome, but too dark and muscular to be my type. He is half-Indian (his mother is Ojibura) and his hair is almost black. He also seemed a little on the young side. Actually he is one month younger than I.

"He knew I was a hooker and accepted the fact. I finally ended up sleeping with him. That was two and half years ago and I had his baby daughter three months ago. He is the first man I've ever been so physically attracted to. He looks even better with his clothes off.

"He is five feet eight inches tall and beautifully muscled. The sun turns him dark bronze in the summer and his skin has the look and feel of expensive velvet. Every inch of him is as hard as stone, and the hair on his chest is fine and forms a cross from collarbone to navel, and nipple to nipple. His face and body are perfectly contoured. He could really put Michelangelo's David to shame.

"He has a behind that a lot of women would trade their souls for and it turns me on to the point of being uncomfortably excited. When he walks around the house nude I usually end up cornering him in the bedroom. He wears body shirts and tight bell-bottomed trousers especially for me. Even a little thing like a few curls showing through an open neckline or taut muscles moving under the fabric of his slacks turns me on fiercely. He's beautifully hung. We measured and he is five inches in length and four and a half in circumference when flaccid. Fully erect his penis measures seven and a half inches in length and five and a half in circumference.

"Not one word of my description is false. Bill is the answer to most girls' dreams. In fact, most of the women he meets have no qualms about inviting him to bed before they even know him. He has a full-time job now as a tire builder which keeps those muscles hard, but he is still a part-time bartender, and as I sometimes go with him for a few drinks on Saturday night, I've had opportunity to see women make out-and-out physical passes at him. They even pinch his behind!"

I don't know what effect that description has on you, but I can feel myself responding to Iris's arousal though I have no part in that arousal. Somehow she has managed to impart the sexual impact that Bill's body has on her. She not only responds to his physical appeal, but, like a male, translates the physical into the cerebral.

I have always contended that what Dr. Reuben describes as "fun-sex," i.e., sex purely for the physical sensations, is far inferior to the experience of lovemaking, where physical sex is used to convey to the partner, and he/she to you, the depth of the emotional love you feel for one another. If there isn't actual love, then at least, the very least, there must be feelings of respect and regard for one another. If neither love nor respect are present then taking part in sex is purely animal fucking, which I believe is degrading to the cerebral, rational creatures that men and women are. This means that the one-night stand is out, as is true promiscuity— sex with anyone who happens to be along—because there must be an emotional relationship of sorts; and such a relationship can only be built up over a number of contacts, for only very rarely is there instantaneous emotional accord.

It has long been the universally held view that the male is more promiscuously minded than the female and that he is so because of his easy and quick physical response to sexual stimuli, while the female, whose responses are very much slower and capricious, places a far greater value on the emotional side of a sexual relationship than on the physical. Put more briefly, a man can fuck, enjoy himself, and forget, whereas for a woman each experience has a significance which makes it difficult, if not impossible, for her to fuck unless she has an emotional regard for her partner.

When one considers the scientific analysis of human sexual response, however, this seems to be the very opposite of what should happen. On the one side you have Kinsey quite correctly stating that the male's physical responses are mostly the outcome of psychological stimuli while the woman physically responds chiefly to physiologic stimuli, and on the other side that the male's experience is more significantly physical than psychological while the female's experience is an emotional experience rather than a physical one.

Since I began this study, I am coming to conclude more and more that though the scientific analysis as

43

stated by Kinsey is right, in the past the woman's responses to physical stimuli have not been sufficiently taken into account, nor the fact that just like the man she is aroused to physical response by the psychological stimuli into which she translates her physical stimuli. I think the chief difference between male and female response is that the male is unaware of the psychological stimuli because his physical responses are so obvious—it is absolutely impossible to ignore a hard-on—whereas the female is aware of her psychological stimuli because she cannot achieve them without deliberate physical stimuli. Even from the statements I have already given, this seems to me to emerge very plainly, and the statements that follow will serve to underline it.

Betty lives in Los Angeles, California. She is sixteen and in high school. "I can't tell you my address because I don't want my parents to know I wrote to you. They would be very mad."

She says: "The way some boys look does turn me on. Boys with long hair look great, and also if they have a moustache or a small beard. The boys that attract me are tall and not fat. They look great wearing jeans and clothes like that. They look great not wearing a shirt. Their muscles turn me on. Most of my boy friends are good at sports. It turns me on a whole bunch if they wear tight pants so I can see where their cock and balls are."

Though only sixteen, Betty has had sexual experiences, and already she responds to visual stimuli, as the rest of her answers, which I shall be quoting later, unconsciously emphasize. In fact, the greatest part of her responses are derived from visual stimuli. She left blank my second question which asked, "Other male qualities, if appearance does not turn you on."

One might be tempted to argue that in early adolescence the physical rather than the psychological is much more likely to predominate, since the first impression of fucking is that it is a purely physical activity and so does petting to arousal seem to be. But see what Lynne, who lives in New York says, and she is twenty-six.

"If a man were attractive to me in many other ways but was not physically attractive, I could not be aroused by him. I will try to describe the kind of physical appearance that is arousing to me. Facially, I like a man who looks rugged but not coarse. I do not like a man with a baby face. He must have blue eyes and hair that is thick and wavy. His hair must be well-styled and not real long or shaggy. He must be taller than I am (I'm five feet seven in my bare feet), and he should not be visibly underweight or overweight. I like a man who looks sturdy and muscular, but I don't like a man who looks like a muscleman. I especially like a man with broad shoulders and a large chest.

"There are also little things that make a difference to me. I like a man whose hands look strong, and who has long fingers. It also arouses me for a man to have a good amount of hair on his body, but he should not be overly hairy. It's especially arousing for me if he has a good amount of hair on his chest, and he has a thick growth of pubic hair.

"One thing that is very important to me is the shape of a man's bottom. A well-shaped bottom is one of the first things I look for in a man. It should be round and firm and not too large. One other thing that is important to me is that he have good teeth. I can't stand a man whose teeth look bad when he smiles."

Jeanne is an airline stewardess who lives in New York. She is twenty-seven and has been married for two years. She had her first homosexual experience last summer, but all of her other sexual experiences have been with men. "I do feel sexually aroused by men and women alike, but have a strong preference for men." She and her husband have a very free relationship. As she is away from home so much, both recognize that they are equally entitled to extramarital affairs.

"*Physical appearance.* I prefer older men. I do not feel, and never have felt, strong sexual desires for men younger than I, or even of my own age. I am turned on most thoroughly by a man's eyes. I enjoy having men look at me straight in the eyes and I am extremely aroused by eye contact. I feel a certain amount of frankness in a man who can look at me directly. And I definitely like frankness and honesty about sex. I have had men I do not know tell me quite abruptly that they would like to sleep with me. I have never been put off by this sort of thing. I may not take them up on the offer—and then again I may—but I would certainly never put a man down for this sort of boldness. And, in addition, whether I responded to the offer or not, I always feel quite turned on by such an encounter.

"I am five eight and I strongly prefer men taller than I. I am very turned on by facial hair—beards, moustaches—but I like for them to be clean and not matted or dirty looking. I am aroused by airline pilots in uniform.

"On second thoughts, physical appearance is really not important to me. I like certain physical characteristics in a man, but I would certainly never sleep with a man because of his looks. I did this one time and found it an empty experience. I like men I can talk to. I can find men who want to share much of themselves with me and who enjoy having me do the same. It is with these men—and only with these—that I also share sex."

Blatantly physical is Janet, of London, England. She is twenty-three, unmarried, middle-class, and educated at a large boarding school for girls.

"Naturally I like a man to be good-looking and attractive. I like him to be at least five nine to six feet. I am particularly attracted to young men between eighteen and twenty-five. They should be strong and manly, but not muscular. I like their hair to be long, but not below the shoulders. I do not like 'butch' types.

"I do not like men with hairy chests and legs, and those with hair on their stomachs. I like men with soft and smooth skins and with a minimum of pubic hair, particularly on their testicles. I prefer men to be uncircumcised, first, because I think the uncircumcised penis is more attractive to look at, both in erection and otherwise, than the circumcised one, and secondly, because I find the uncircumcised penis is far more sexually exciting, particularly in hand masturbation and fellatio, both of which practices I enjoy.

"I find from my experience that young men are not very keen on cunnilingus, or even full sexual intercourse. I find that most young men are satisfied by some tongue-kissing and then being wanked off, or sucked off without anything further. *To me, this is all I want, and it gives me the most wonderful orgasms.* [My italics—R.C.] If one of them should want to fuck me or suck me off, so much the better.

"What really turns me on is the feeling of holding a young man's erect penis in my hand, particularly if he is uncircumcised, and then to pull and slide his foreskin backwards and forwards until he comes—in other words to wank him off. I love seeing him come, and I love the feel of his semen on my fingers. Better still, of course, I love sucking a young man's penis, particularly again if he is uncircumcised, and sucking him until he comes, and I love taking his whole ejaculation in my mouth. Although the semen gives me a slight burning feeling in the throat, I love its salty taste. *Whilst wanking or sucking off a young man, I have the most delicious orgasms without him even touching me.* [My italics—R.C.]

"When I was about seventeen I met a very attractive young soldier who was in a Scottish regiment, and he was wearing a kilt. He took me to a cinema, and after a bit he began kissing me. Then he took my hand and put it on his bare knee. Almost automatically I ran my hand up and under his kilt and took hold of his erect penis. I knew at once that he was uncircumcised, and after feeling and squeezing it he suddenly came into my fingers and I had an orgasm. This was the first time I had ever felt and wanked off a boy.

"Ever since then I have always been attracted by young soldiers wearing kilts or any young man in a kilt. It is also perhaps because the first boy I ever felt and wanked off was uncircumcised that I always love uncircumcised penises as opposed to circumcised ones, although I enjoy both.

"I have found, too, that uncircumcised boys get much more excited when being felt, wanked off, or sucked off than circumcised ones, and they also produce much more lubricating juice before they actually come, which excites me. I have known circumcised penises which remain quite dry until just before the moment of coming, but this never happens with uncircumcised ones."

I said that Janet is blatantly physical, and so she is at first sight. But please glance again at the two sentences I have put into italics. She has orgasms without being touched by her partner. This is what is known as psychic orgasm, and is produced by the psychological stimuli. This is rare in women, but does frequently occur in younger men, who are able to fantasize to orgasm. Exactly how Janet translates the physical stimuli of observing an uncircumcised penis ejaculating under her hand into a psychological stimulus so intense that she produces an orgasm in herself I cannot explain since she is unable to identify her thought processes in this situation. But she exhibits what have been regarded as plainly male characteristics all along the line.

"Here's a bit of background first," says Joanna, who lives in Scotland. "I'm twenty-four, Vic, my husband, twenty-two, and we just got married last November though we lived together as man and wife two years before that. We love each other a lot and didn't really need to get married to prove anything—just for formalities and legality. We have a fairly open marriage; that is, it hasn't been put to any strain yet, but we both agree that we are perfectly free to do what we want. I have had an old lover when Vic was away and it was not important.

"I do get turned on by a man's physical appearance. There is a certain type of man I find very attractive. He has a hard-to-describe certain softness in the face—not feminine. Masculine, yet tender. And not skinny. Being fat myself I like well-built men. And, of course, a bulging cock in his trousers always makes me go on heat.

"Yes, appearance does matter initially, but I can love a man, once I know him, who is not good-looking."

One of the things that has faintly surprised me is the large number of women who claim to be aroused by the bulge in a man's trousers. Clearly, this was appreciated by fifteenth, sixteenth, and seventeenth century males who wore the codpiece, despite what my encyclopedia says the reason for its use was.

CODPIECE: Name for bagged appendage, sometimes loose, sometimes in the form of a flap, to the
hose or breeches worn by men during the 15th to
17th centuries, cod being a term, no longer in current
usage, for the scrotum. Often conspicuous and orna-
mental, the codpiece was made necessary by the tightness of the garments of the period.

Maybe the tightness of the garments did make it
necessary, but why accentuate and decorate it if
the real object was not to draw the woman's attention and her imagination to the bulge?

There is a widespread idea that women do not
require any stimulus analogous to that which her
breasts provide the male. Perhaps when looser
breeches and trousers were in vogue and the man's
genital bulge could not be seen, women were
thought not to be interested visually because they
were not visually stimulated. But women *are* visually stimulated, and now that fashion has brought
back the tight trousers, we find that interest in the
"bulge" has only been latent.

Maxine, who is English, twenty-four, and single,
says, "A man's physical appearance does matter to
me. He must look clean and be smartly dressed (or
at least neatly dressed). The tighter his trousers the
better, so that it is possible to see the outline of his
penis. I'm also aroused when I see a hairy body—
not too much though, because that has the opposite
effect."

Doreen, twenty-four, heterosexual, upper-mid-
dle-class English family, university education, get-

ting married this year, and who says, "Very, very happy about sex—best thing since sliced bread," asserts, "To sleep with a man I need to have a lot of female and personality qualities catered for. So I like big shoulders and strong arms to protect me, and sensitive, gentle, *clean* hands to caress me, and a mouth that smiles readily to amuse me.

"But to react purely sexually I get more basic. *Narrow hips and hard buttocks, with tight trousers and the genitals worn proudly, will turn me on even for men whom I otherwise regard as weak. . . .*"

Carol is forty-six and lives in Washington, D.C. She is married but her marriage is breaking up. "During the past year while I was discovering my sexuality, he was losing whatever sexual power he had.

"Until recently I would not have admitted that a man's physical appearance rouses me sexually. I had always been taught that nice girls do not react that way to a man. When I did react that way to a boy or man, I repressed my feelings because they made me feel like I was being bad. In the past year or so, I have changed a lot, mainly due to *Forum*, and now I can accept the fact that some men's physical appearance does rouse me sexually, without feeling bad about it.

"The first thing I notice about a man is his general build and the way he carries himself. . . . The next thing . . . I also notice his eyes. . . . If I like a man's face I look more closely at his body. The more athletic his body looks, the better I like it. Most of all I notice his legs. If they look strong, and if some of the movement of his leg muscles shows through his pants as he walks, it probably means that the rest of his body is in good shape, too. That does not mean that I like men with big, bulging muscles. Men like that always seem a little 'queer' to me. It is still rather embarrassing to admit it, but the one place I do look for a bulge is in front of a man's pants. I am curious about what is producing that bulge. That does not mean that the bigger the bulge, the more I like it. It means that I think it's sexy for there to be some bulge showing there."

Jan says, "I am twenty-three, single, a university student, American, good-looking, strictly heterosexual, very liberal, and well-traveled."

Though I am, at the moment, concentrating on the main bulge, I propose to give the background information Jan has given me, because although she failed to provide a return address, she is clearly a very interesting person sexually.

"I first had sex at sixteen. I have never had sex for money. Sex for me has usually been out of desire, a few times out of compassion for the guy, and a few times out of curiosity. I have had sex with 69 [a symbolic figure?—R.C.]; 61 were white, 7 were black, and 2 were orientals. Of the 69 men, 24 were American, 16 Canadian, 4 Italian, 10 Spanish, 5 British, and one each from Poland, Jamaica, Switzerland, Mexico, Puerto Rico, Cuba, Colombia, Germany, Morocco, Austria, and the Philippines. As you see, I keep a diary [but can't add up, because all those come to 70—R.C.] My sex partners have all been under thirty. For several years now I have never even accepted dates from guys that I would not be willing to consider as sex partners. . . ."

[I do hope that all this is not just a lovely fantasy.]

"*Physical appearance.* Very definitely. Both clothed and unclothed; I cannot be excited by a guy who is not clean. Bad breath, yellow cigarette stains on hands, a couple of days' growth of beard, all turn me off. A beard can only turn me on if neat and black.

"My sexy male would be over five feet nine inches tall, shaggy hair, preferably black; clean swimmer's build, and would be wearing a sweater and rather *tight pants.* A good-looking guy dressed that way would catch my eye and *rouse my feelings by sight alone. Tight pants on a guy which hint of good endowment are stimulating to me.* Unclothed, two more aspects can rouse me: hair—pubic and on chest is exciting (I was most turned off by the Moroccan when I saw all body hair shaved) and large endowment is most stimulating visually. A smaller penis can be quite stimulating in action. But the sight of a large organ on a guy is rousing in itself."

Meg doesn't give her age, but she lives in London. In answer to my question, "Are you sexually roused by a man's physical appearance?" she replied simply, "If I can see the bulge in his trousers."

Sheila is thirty-two, married for seven years, and with her husband and two children lives in Newcastle-on-Tyne, England. She says she has always been turned on by slim, very dark males.

"Jet black hair on the head and belly against a

dark olive skin arouses me at first glance. Maybe this is because the first boy I ever saw completely naked, when I was fifteen—he was sixteen—was my Spanish sister-in-law's brother. He had thick black shiny hair on his head, so black that it had green lights in it, and the hair covering his belly was a mass of lovely black curls. His skin was almost the colour of olives. I don't know whether you have noticed, but skin of this colour nearly always shines like silk. I thought at first it was a kind of natural grease which the skin produced, but later I found that it wasn't. But it's much smoother and sensuously sexy to stroke than any other coloured skin.

"I'd never seen a boy's cock or his balls before in the flesh, but it wasn't they that attracted my attention first, it was his hair and skin. It was only when I realised that I was so turned on that I was dripping wet between my legs, that I noticed his penis and testicles. He hadn't a hard-on and his penis was one of the most beautifully proportioned I've ever seen, long, fairly slender, the skin of the shaft slightly darker than his body skin, and the skin covering the head was the deep purple of an aubergine skin. It was a very hot day, and his balls hung slack and heavy, and when he moved, they and his cock swayed from side to side.

"He passed his hand across his face and said in his careful English, 'It is very hot, is it not?' I couldn't answer him, I just nodded. 'Are you coming to swim also?' he asked me. (I've forgotten to say that I had taken him for a walk by the river, and when we had come to a secluded spot, he had suddenly said, 'I think I swim', and had at once begun to take his clothes off.) 'Good,' he said, and dived into the river.

"I had never been seen naked by a boy before, either. At least, I had been seen by my brother once. He's eight years older than I am. He had come into the bathroom just as I was getting into the bath. He gave me a terrible wigging afterwards for not locking the bathroom door. He was an awful prude. I could never fathom why he married Eva. She's brought him out a bit, but he hasn't entirely lost his prudishness. (I hope I'm not going on too long.)

"Well, I didn't give a thought for that either, and began to take off my clothes. He was a good swimmer, and I couldn't take my eyes off him, and the water passing over his body was more exciting still. By the time I was naked I was bursting with desire. I just couldn't help myself. I sat down on the grass and pretended I was taking off my shoes, but with my other hand I touched myself, and in about ten seconds I exploded. It was so intense, I was trembling from head to foot.

"He shouted to me to go in, and I called back that I was coming, but I couldn't move until the trembling had died down a little. Then I walked into the river, because I didn't want to get my hair wet.

" 'You are beautiful,' he called. 'Thank you,' I said. 'You are very beautiful, too!' 'I am very pleased you think so.'

"We swam about for a bit, and then lay down in the grass to dry in the sun, because we hadn't any towels. He lay on his back with his eyes closed and I lay not far away, unable to take my eyes off him. I don't know whether he realised I was looking at him or not, but after a minute or two he began to play with his penis, and in seconds, it seemed, he had a hard-on and was rubbing it with his hand. It wasn't very much bigger than when it had been soft, but I was surprised by the change that came over it. Looking back on this incident, I always wonder why I wasn't afraid that he would want to come in me, and I knew enough to know that if he did, I might have a baby. But neither the thought nor fear came into my head.

"Then he opened his eyes and saw I was looking at him and grinned. 'Would you like to do it for me?' he asked. 'I've never done it before,' I told him. 'It is not difficult. See. Do like that.' So I did as he showed me, and he closed his eyes again. Once he told me not to grip his penis so hard. The lubrication poured out of his penis in a continuous stream, which made the skin under my hand smoother than silk. Presently, he began to breathe hard, and his lips drew back from his teeth. Then he let out a loud 'Aah' and arched his back, and the semen shot out, and it caught in the hair in his belly in little pearls, and hung there twinkling.

"He told me to stop when his cock stopped throbbing. I was all on fire again, and didn't know what to do. But he said, 'Shall I do it for you? It is much nicer when someone does it for you? Shall I? I do it with a girl at home. I like it this way, because I do not wish to make a girl have a baby.'

57

"He put his hand between my legs and grinned. 'Good,' he said. 'You are very wet. You want it, yes?' I nodded, and he began to finger my clitoris, as he leaned over me and sucked one of my nipples. I did not come quite so quickly this time, and he didn't seem to know I had. I was going to tell him when I felt the sensations building up again. I didn't take his hand away until I had come another three times. 'Was it good?' he asked. 'Oh, yes!' I said. 'I was right, you see. It is much better, isn't it? Shall we do it again tomorrow?' 'If you like,' I said.

"But we didn't do it again the next day. We never did it again, because during the night the weather broke, and the day after that he went home. He didn't come to England again for three years, by which time life had changed.

"I began masturbating just before I was twelve, and I used to do it nearly every day. After Felipe went home, I did it several times a day, and every time I used to picture him, and it was so vivid, it was as if he was there with me. One day I came off fifteen times.

"By the time Felipe came to visit us again, I was no longer a virgin. (I was working in the town and had my own flat.) The first one, Roy, was a nice boy, with black hair, but not so thick as Felipe's, and his skin wasn't so dark either. We used to make love about once a week. I had fitted myself up with a diaphragm as I wasn't sure about the Pill, and had great faith in it, so I wasn't afraid of getting pregnant. Roy's techniques were not too bad for a novice, but do you know, Dr. Chartham, I never once came off with him, though we were together for nine months.

"Then Roy went away, and we didn't meet very often, so I formed a relationship with Peter. He was one of the handsomest men I've ever seen. He was brunette and though the hair on his head, under his arms, and his bush were very thick, he hadn't a hair on his chest, and there was a sort of down on his belly. He was only about five feet nine inches, but he had a magnificent penis even when it was soft, and very big and heavy balls. When he had an erection his penis was just over seven inches long, but it was so thick that, honestly, I couldn't take it in my mouth. When he came in you, you knew it. He was seven years older than I, and he'd been around a bit. He really did enjoy making love and he easily qualified to be a Sensuous Man.

"Yet I had the same trouble with him. To say I came off every fourth fuck, is probably an over-estimate, though I could actually feel his penis doing something to my clitoris. I would get to a certain point, and seldom get beyond it. Peter and I stayed together for nearly two years, having it off about twice a week. Then one day he asked me to marry him. I said I would think about it. He said no, he wanted an answer on the spot. So I said no. I never saw him again, except occasionally in the pub. He soon got shacked up with another girl, whom he eventually married. He had a really glorious body, and yet it never really turned me on.

"I had the opportunity of shacking up with another boy soon afterwards, but I thought I would wait a while. Then my sister-in-law told me Felipe would be visiting us again, and I decided to wait the two or three months until he arrived, just in case he wanted to make love to me, and this time properly.

"Truly, I cannot describe what I felt when I watched him undressing. He had grown quite a bit, and filled out, and, as I recalled it, his penis was bigger, too. The hair all over his body was thicker than ever, and it seemed that his skin was darker and silkier than I had remembered it.

"He wasn't so expert as Peter, but he didn't have to be. I came off during loveplay. I came off as soon as he came in me, and while he was bringing himself off, I came again and again. So it was, every time we made love. We got into trouble with my brother, because Felipe spent most of his time with me. But my sister-in-law put things right. I think she hoped we would marry. But though sex with him was so fantastic, I knew I wasn't in love with him.

"To cut a long story short, over the next six years I had three or four affairs. I hadn't cottoned on to the fact that I could only truly get turned on by a dark-haired boy with olive skin, and I had a variety of colourings. One was a handsome Swede who had a sexual stamina and an imagination to match, greater even than Peter's. But it was the old story. When we coupled I rarely came off, and he could only bring me off orally now and again, until I discovered that if I closed my eyes, and imagined he was Felipe, it would happen in no time. At first

I was a little bit frightened of this. This was the first time I wrote to you, remember? I thought I was turning kinky, and I didn't want to be. You'll never know how grateful I am to you for putting me right.

"Well, then I met my husband, Ricco. He's Italian, three years older than me and he part-owns a restaurant. I went in one morning before they were open for lunch, to book a table for dinner that evening with a friend. He was in his shirt-sleeves, and his shirt was open, and peeping through was a mass of the loveliest black curls you've seen. The hair on his head was very thick and naturally wavy, and his skin, though not quite so olive as Felipe's, was beautiful. I was so turned on, I could hardly tell him what I wanted.

"He wasn't there that evening, but I just couldn't get him out of my mind. Then I started going there regularly for lunch, and in no time at all we were having an affair. The first time, I could have been with Felipe, I came off so often. But I was aware of a great difference. Ricco is the kindest, gentlest man I know, and above all, thoughtful. Where Felipe had just got down to it, Ricco asked if it was being good for me, was I comfortable, did I like this, did I like that. Even Peter had never been so considerate. I think I fell in love with him that first night, and every time it got better. So when he asked me to marry him, I said, yes, please, quickly! That was seven years ago, and there has been no change, except for the better, in our sexual and other relationship. There is scarcely a time that we make love when I don't have multi-orgasms. I adore every hair on his body, and square inch of his skin, and I love him for being the truly kind man he is."

This is, of course, a classic illustration of one of the manifestations of human attraction. In the great majority of cases, the initial attraction is physical. Only later does the psychic attraction come into existence, and the two types of attraction together create love, or, at least, the breeding ground for love. I am not convinced by the concept of platonic love. In my view, there must be a fusion of the two attractions before a lasting and meaningful relationship can emerge. It is certainly true that a lasting and meaningful relationship cannot be based on physical attraction only; and it must be equally true that psychic attraction alone cannot secure the survival of a relationship, except in very exceptional cases. Usually when it happens, the sex-drive and libido of *both* partners is very low. Then the psychic may compensate to some extent for the lack of the physical.

Sheila's account demonstrates the powerful influence that "imprinting" can have throughout one's life. A first experience can fashion one's behavior and reactions throughout the rest of the life-span. This is particularly true of the first shared sexual experience, and it is on account of this that I am so vigorously opposed to the honeymoon and especially to the tradition that a marriage should be consummated on the first night. It is also on this account that I urge all young people not to attempt full lovemaking until they can arrange comfortable surroundings secure from the risk of interruptions, and time enough not to make it a hurried experience. It is on this account that I impress on parents, if it is at all possible, not to have their young children in bedrooms next to their own, where they may hear, through the thin walls, the sounds of parents making love. And it is on this account, that I beg parents to take precautions against their young children ever witnessing the "primal scene," i.e., witnessing parents actually engaged in lovemaking, at an age when they are too young to understand what is happening.

Those who work in this field, will tell you that the sexual lives of large numbers of men and women have been ruined by the first shared sexual experience being a disaster. Though it can be done, it is a very difficult process to remove the effects of a bad experience which has made a lasting impression.

Lucille is twenty, and lives in Orlando, Florida.

"When I was about sixteen, someone had told me that you can tell the size of a man's cock from the size of his nose, and from then on, I went mad on noses. It was the first thing I looked at, and then I would look down at his bulge, if he had one. If he had a big nose and his bulge was promising, too, I'd get turned on in no time, just imagining what his cock would be like. Then I had this experience.

"There was this boy, Gordon. He was a good-looking guy, and had a great sense of humor, and we were attracted to one another the first time we met. And, of course, he had a largish nose and really great bulge. I'd had two or three affairs by this time, though by some quirk of fate, never with a boy with a big nose, though I couldn't complain about their cocks.

"When it became obvious that Gordon wanted to lay me, I got really excited. Now I was going to find out what a really large cock could do to a gal. I didn't need a second invitation to go to his pad. He didn't make a pass at me at once, and we sat on the sofa and drank bourbon and listened to the record player. After the second drink, he made a start. I was already turned on in anticipation and began touching him up, too. Just as I was going to unzip his fly, he excused himself to go to the bathroom.

"When he came back, I went straight for his fly. When I put my hand in, I was puzzled. His cock was so small I could hardly feel it, though it was stiff. I realized then, why he'd gone to the bathroom. That promising bulge must have mostly been padding. I hadn't thought guys would play such a trick, and for a moment it quite turned me off. But I wasn't turned off for long, because he obviously knew what pleased women, and when we eventually got down to it, that little cock did things to me that the bigger ones hadn't.

"But the incident put me off noses. They don't turn me on any more. Now I go for really small, tight asses. It's fantastic what the feel of them does for me if I put my hands on them after the guy has come in me, and he's bucking away. They get wonderful dimples in them. Sometimes a guy will let me fix up mirrors, or do it in front of a mirror so that I can see his ass and the dimples while we're having it off. I still haven't had it with a really big cock though."

Sharon is twenty-four, married, with one child. Her husband is a salesman based in Racine, Wisconsin. They have been married for three years and though Roy is away several nights of the week, they couldn't have a happier sex-life, she says.

"Am I turned on by a man's looks? I don't mind about whether he has handsome features or not, but I first look at his eyes, and if there is a twinkle in them I know he must be a nice guy with a sense of humor. A sense of humor in a guy is essential to me, otherwise I have difficulty in responding.

"Next I look at his mouth. If his lips are thin and straight, I know he'll be a bit of a prude and if we ever come to it, will disapprove of some of the things I like. If his lips are full (not flabby), deep red, and moist, then I know he'll be a really good lover to me. You see, I go wild about cunnilingus, and the thought of what that beautiful mouth will do to me turns me on sky-high in seconds.

"Perhaps it's my imagination that men with thin lips can't give head so well as men with full lips. I often wonder if this is a kink of mine. Do other women get turned on, or off, by men's mouths?"

Glenda is a fairly high-powered executive in a department store in London, England. She is twenty-seven, a career woman, and unmarried.

"I'm afraid I get turned on most by young boys. I prefer boys of fifteen, but as the law is against boys of that age fucking, I have to be content with sixteen-year-olds. What arouses me is their fresh complexions and young, hard, firm bodies. They're not heavy with muscles yet, and they're not paunchy, and at that age they have a sexual stamina which boys even a year or two older do not have. At least that's my impression, and my experience, but perhaps I've been lucky in my choice of younger partners.

"Then there's their cocky attitude about knowing it all, their despondency when they find they don't, and their gratitude when you teach them. I've been with older men, who gave the impression of sophistication, and yet didn't really know the first thing about lovemaking, and when in desperation I've taken the lead, they take sexual umbrage, and moan about being made to feel inadequate, which they actually are. But the youngsters never react like this. They are honest enough to know they've something to learn, and enthusiastic about being taught. And their eagerness to please one, I find sexually rousing in itself.

"I suppose I am a pervert, but I'm not depraved. I don't do the boys any harm. In fact, I believe I do them a lot of good, and they keep me balanced and satisfied."

ii. A Naked Male Partner (1) Without (2) With Erection

It is widely believed that women are not visually stimulated by a nude male either without or with an erection. If, however, more than half my sample who are aroused by physical appearance, admit to being physically turned on by "a bulge in the trousers," maybe it is reasonable to suppose that they will react more sexually to the naked male in the same way that the male is sexually roused by the sight of the nude female. But, "they" say, there are many men who are more roused by the scantily clad female, because they have to imagine what the hidden parts look like and so have to bring their psychological apparatus into play. On this analogy, are not your women who are stimulated by The Bulge, the nature of which they have to imagine, less likely to be stimulated by the totally nude male? I can agree that this may happen when the penis is limp and the man not sexually roused, but I would have thought that the sight of a rampant penis, the indisputable sign that a man is sexually roused, and, in a situation that is already a sexual one, the nearness of an aroused man must be arousing to a woman who is not averse to a sexual experience.

Anyway, let's see how it turns out. Let's take first of all those who are sexually roused by physical appearances.

Fourteen out of the 45 are not turned on at all by the nude male body either with or without an erection. The remaining 31 are, with qualifications. Here is a typical selection of what they say.

Susan is nineteen, American, and lives in Cambridge, Massachusetts.

"Yes! What turns me on is helping my partner undress before intercourse. When I see how erect his penis is when I slowly slip his clothes off makes me get ready for the next step. It's really about the same if he hasn't an erection yet, because I know that penis won't stay limp for long."

Madge is seventeen, and lives in Birmingham, England.

"A naked male body only excites me occasionally, and there must be an erection."

Barbara, of Kansas City, is twenty-eight, and has been married ten years.

"Yes, I'm always excited by a nude partner provided he has an erection."

Frances is thirty-six, twice married, and now again divorced; she lives in Denver, Colorado. She at last believes she has found her ideal man, who is not an American. She is very much in love with him.

"As for naked male partners—he's the only one I can bear naked and naked he *never* is without an erection. Sometimes I wish he was—I would like so much to be able to arouse him, and bring him to complete fulfillment myself. This happened only once—when I knew he had to awaken early, and I awoke before him and started him with oral love. But he is so aggressive that he prefers to do all the initiating, and I accept that."

Edith, who lives in Edinburgh, Scotland, is twenty-six, and married, just declared succinctly, "BOTH;" while Bessie of San Francisco, California, who is twenty-nine and very happily married, was almost equally terse, with "Both—I like to see it both ways."

Marilyn is thirty-one, married, and lives in Richmond, Virginia. She says, "It makes no difference whether my nude lover has an erection or not, he still excites me. If he has an erection, it makes me feel good that I contributed to making it that way. If it is not erect, it is a challenge for me to arouse him so that it will be erect."

Of the 153 who are turned on by physical appearances, 14 are unmoved by the naked male with or without an erection, 13 are turned on without erection, 36 by erection only, and 90 by both.

Here are some typical remarks.

"A naked male partner by all means, but not just *any* naked male partner. He has to be my choice and no erection necessary for me to be roused, but if it's there it's wonderful." (American, forty-six, single.)

"A naked male partner with or without erection —yes! If he has an erection, I'm aroused because it's for me. If he hasn't an erection yet, I know I'll soon have things well in hand—or mouth—and he'll soon be erect. Either way it's sexy." (American, twenty-nine, single.)

"Both. The naked male is beautiful with or without an erection. Men are beautiful clothed, partially nude—any way, men are great!" (American, twenty-two, single.)

"A naked male partner with or without erection, *if he is walking around.* His nodding erection is particularly exciting when he walks." (British, twenty-four, married.)

"A naked male, with or without erection, if he has a good body, is very stimulating. With an erection even more so, as it makes me want to handle him. Without an erection I feel more tender, wanting to kiss and caress his balls and limp penis, and the rest of his anatomy." (British, twenty-six, single, permanent relationship with man of thirty-eight, no wish to be married.)

"Yes, a naked male partner with or without erection as long as sex is intended. In some cases a sleeping naked partner." (American, black, thirty-five, single.)

"I am roused by seeing a man naked if he fits my image of a 'sexy' man. I get even more aroused if he does not know I can see him. Seeing him with an erection is even better if it's strong and good-sized. It is very disappointing, and off-turning, to see a 'sexy' man who turns out to have an erection that is weak or small. Watching a man get an erection is best of all, especially if I am the cause of it. When I am with a man and he is nude and he does not have an erection yet, I get roused by watching his penis bounce around and wiggle as he moves." (American, thirty, divorced.)

"I used to think that nice girls did not like to see a naked male. Because of that I was past twenty-one years old before I ever saw a naked man. Now I become very roused if I see a naked man whether or not he has an erection, but I am always curious to see what his penis looks like when erect. Another thing that rouses me sexually is watching a man as his penis erects. The process of erection rouses

me as much as seeing the final result of the process."
(American, forty-six, heading for divorce.)

"What really arouses me is watching his penis
become erect. I especially like it if he is uncircumcised because I get very aroused by watching the
head of his penis emerge from the foreskin." (American, twenty-six, single.)

"My male looks great with or without an erection, but nothing rouses me so quickly as the sight
of him with a rock hard erection pointing to his
chin." (Canadian, twenty-three, married.)

"I only get turned on by seeing an erection if the
penis is quite thin and the guy has nice balls." (English, sixteen, single.)

"Naked males definitely turn me on and I'd like
to see more of them especially with erections. However, I couldn't imagine getting anything out of a
male strip tease. Maybe this is because the appeal
of a female stripper lies largely in the fact that she
is not easily accessible, at least in theory, and this
does not apply to men. Also, I can't imagine anything funnier than men dancing about on stage with
their penises flopping about." (British, twenty-
seven, single.)

"Naked male partner with erection. I go to a
mixed sauna and nudity is quite natural and unsexy
there." (British, twenty-four, married.)

"When I play around with a boy, we aren't always naked. I've only been with a completely naked
boy a few times. It turns me on a whole bunch to
see and feel a boy when he's naked. Or even part
naked. Most of all when his cock is big and hard.

I get really turned on if he has a real big cock. I can't wait to tell my girlfriends about it." (American, sixteen, single.)

"One of the most arousing sights to me is that of my partner naked standing up with a massive erection, or even more than that, I love to get them to wank in front of me. Then when they're nearly coming, I'll suck them. (Makes my insides go all a-tremble just writing about it! Phew!!)" (British, nineteen, single.)

"A naked male without an erection. For me its being innocent, easier and more fun to play with and kiss. I like to be able to bring him to an erection when I want it. Even my own husband scares me sometimes when getting undressed and I see he is already erect.

"My feelings, I'm sure, stem from the fact that going to work late at night on the bus, men would expose themselves fully erect, waiting for my reaction. To me it was disgusting not exciting. When I bring my husband to erection by playing with him, everything has a different tone." (American, twenty-two, married.)

These replies, as you see, vary in emphasis on the arousal potential of the erect penis, but there is underlying the statements a definite admission that even when a limp penis has a stimulating effect, it is usually because the woman has the power to bring it to erection, and that when it is erect, it is erect for her. After these replies, let no one tell me that the average uninhibited woman does not react readily to visual stimuli providing her personal standards of male "sexiness" are complied with. But let this twenty-three-year-old, single, American university student have the last word, because as she has perceived it is not quite so white and black as the statements may have seemed to imply.

"This is by far the most difficult of your questions for me to answer. [She is Jan, by the way, who has laid 70 men.] I neither know where to begin nor how to sort out my feelings. Further, as I understood the question, it is not limited to any one sense (i.e. sight) but may include any or all. I wonder also, how literally I should take the use of the word 'partner' as opposed to 'man' in the question. The best I can do is hope to abandon logic and accurately give my feelings.

"In my experience most men have some sort of hang-up (or need reassurance) on two factors—penis size and circumcision. Men that I have known have apologized for, sought assurance about, lamented over every possible combination of these two factors. To the best of my knowledge I have never said anything that would heighten the insecurity of the partner. I believe most men take these factors in terms of 'yes or no,' 'black or white.' I, on the other hand, do not think that many women take these issues in such absolute terms. This is my objective consideration, now to the substantive elements.*

---

* Only three women of the 198 referred to penis size, and these three claimed that they could only be aroused by "enormous cocks." (Two American, one British.) The rest, however, did insist that to be really arousing the erections must be "rock hard."

"The naked male is always interesting but I doubt if I could ever be roused by the sight of a naked male that I had not already fallen for. [This is the general consensus.] Once while studying with a male friend in a house of college students, a good-looking but quite drunk guy appeared in a jock-strap, and was bragging that his organ was enough to scare any girl. He proceeded to lay it upon the table in front of me. Granted that it was a perfect organ, it did not rouse me, and I was not more tempted to accept than if he had not done it.

"That having been said, I must confess that I look forward to and enjoy the sight of a naked partner. [Back to the objective.] But I do not believe the naked male is erotic in the way many men think they are. [Subjective again.] I find the sight of a naked male much more rousing when it is the first time I have seen that man in the nude. After the first time sight plays a lesser role in arousal. The sight of some naked male partners has aroused and excited me greatly, while there were some that af-fected me little.

"(a) Without erection. If I had my choice, I would always prefer to see my partner for the first time without an erection than with one. A good-looking partner with a well-equipped nonerect organ is a joy to see for the first time. It is very rousing to watch or help it go from soft to hard. A small organ is not exciting to look at. I prefer a circumcised penis for sex and I find a circumcised organ is al-ways erotic to look at, but I admit that some uncir-cumcised organs can be very beautiful.

"A well-formed uncircumcised organ in which the skin covers the head has an innocent look, and a certain mystery or mystique about it. It makes me want to feel it and play with it and expose the head. On the other hand, some uncircumcised penises can be very unstimulating to sight, especially if the skin is swollen or too tight to do anything with. I find that even though a perfect uncircumcised penis can have a special attraction at first, this feeling of special attraction tends to disappear on subsequent occasions. I have found myself hoping at times that a given boy would have a large, uncircumcised penis, and at times when it was so I felt it was a special treat. My present partner falls into that category, but the attraction has worn off. Finally, I always find it rousing to caress a penis into erection.

"(b) With erection. Always rousing to the feel. But less rousing to the sight. Certainly much more useful than a soft organ, but much less beautiful to look at. I always feel a bit cheated if the penis is erect the first time I behold it."

*   *   *   *

"I had seen pictures and statues of male nudes which had not made me feel a little bit randy. There was one exception—Rodin's *The Kiss*. The texture of the stone so attracted me that I had to touch it, and when I did, the sensation was so fantastic, I thought this must be what a man's skin feels like, and the more I stroked it, the more turned on I became. The eroticism of the group, the pose, I mean, didn't strike me then. It has since, but I am still not turned on by it, but even if I see a picture of it now, the memory of the feel of the stone brings me on in seconds. But this isn't answering your question.

"As I say, I had seen pictures and statues and so had an idea what the soft penis looked like. I knew that when a man was said to have an erection, his penis got hard and bigger, but I didn't know how hard or how much bigger, so I was not prepared for the first erection I saw.

"I went to university, aged eighteen, still a virgin. More than that, I had *never* had a sexual contact with any boy. My mother was one of those sexually disappointed women, and had tried her best to put my sister and me off men. My sister was two years older than me, and I imagine she was highly sexed. She was taught to masturbate by a friend at school when she was eighteen, and when I came on her doing it at home, and I asked her what she was doing she explained and said she would show me how to do it. We shared a room, and during the holidays we used to masturbate one another almost every night.

"She was more adventurous than me. I suppose it was because she had this high sex-drive. But she used to talk about sex and men with the girls in her class at school, and when we were together she used to tell me about what they said.

"At the beginning of one holiday—she must have been seventeen—she told me that her best friend Elsie H. had been with a boy during the last holidays, and Elsie had said it had been fantastic, indescribably better than when they masturbated one another, and that, said my sister, was pretty good. 'When we do it together, you and me, it's good, isn't it?' she said and I agreed.

" 'I can't understand why Mum keeps dinning it into us that sex isn't nice and that men are horrid, can you?' she went on. 'Perhaps she's never done what we do?' I suggested. 'Well, I'm going to try it with a boy,' she said.

"I was horrified. 'Supposing you have a baby!' I exclaimed. 'There's something boys can wear so that you don't. I'll see Cyril has one of those,' she said.

"Two or three evenings later, she asked Mum if she could go to the cinema with Elsie. Curiously, Mum liked Elsie and said yes, but to come straight home. What she would have said if she'd known that Elsie had already lost her virginity I can't imagine. I was in bed, reading, when my sister came home.

"I could see she was excited. 'I've done it!' she whispered. 'What was it like?' I asked. 'I can't tell you. It was out of this world!' she answered. 'Didn't it hurt? It's supposed to hurt first time,' I said. 'I didn't tell you,' she said, 'but when I made up my mind to do it, I got one of those thick candles from the school chapel and put it inside me. That hurt, but Elsie said it wouldn't hurt any more. I'm going to do it again as often as I can.'

"Next morning she asked Mum if she could ask Cyril to tea on Sunday. Mum nearly went through the roof. She was certainly not going to have boys in her house, and if she ever found out that either

of us was having anything to do with boys, she'd
. . . she'd . . .

"During the next summer holidays, my sister's
period was late, and she thought she was pregnant.
I said I didn't see how she could be if Cyril wore a
rubber, but she said the time before last, he'd stayed
in her until his thing had gone soft, and when he
took it out, they found the rubber had come off. For
the next four or five days, my sister was sick with
worry, weeping most of the time, and not eating.
Mum didn't seem to be worried. She said girls of
her age sometimes got depressed like that. But it was
terrible to see my sister in the state she was in, and
I think that's what made me not have sex myself,
though I would have liked to have tried it. Anyway, my sister wasn't pregnant. Her period eventually started.

"I hope you don't mind all these details. I thought
they might interest you.

"Well, as I've said, I was still a virgin when I
went to college, and I hadn't seen a boy naked, and
even not petted with one. There was a boy, a fresh-
man like me, whom I used to sit next to in lectures.
We got friendly, and he asked me to go out with
him. I liked him very much, so I agreed. Though he
boarded in college, his parents lived in one of the
suburbs.

"One Saturday afternoon, about half-term, it was
a lovely warm summer day, and we hired a punt.
When we came off the river about six, Kit said he
had to go home to see if the house was all right,
because his parents were away for the weekend.

78

Would I like to go with him? We could have a fry-up for supper, which would be a change from the nosh we got in college. I thought it was a great idea.

"When we got to the house we were both thirsty, and Kit got us gins and orange. We drank the first one rather quickly, because we were so thirsty. The house was stuffy, because the windows hadn't been opened for a couple of days, and Kit had taken off his shirt and was just in a pair of white shorts. When he had poured out a second drink, he said he thought he would open the bedroom windows and asked me if I'd like to see his bedroom. So, drinks in hand, we went upstairs. His parents must have been very comfortably off, because it was a large house, five bedrooms and three bathrooms, and it was beautifully furnished, mostly with antiques.

"We opened all the windows in the other rooms before we went to his room. It was a sort of study-bedroom, and I learned more about him in five minutes in that room than I had in the five weeks or so I had known him. He had quite a large library, and I stood looking at the books, he came up behind me and kissing the nape of my neck, he put an arm round me and his hand over a breast. I went weak at the knees, and had a desperate desire to kiss him, so I turned to him, put my arm round him, and kissed him. My hand touched the skin of his back. The sensation was even more arousing than when I had stroked the Rodin, and the sensations lower down were more exciting than when my sister stimulated me.

"The next thing I knew we were lying on his bed, with me in just my panties, and he in his shorts. The contact of his skin with mine was even more arousing, but it was our kisses—which I now know were deep kisses—that brought me almost to the point of climax. He put his hand inside my panties, and the skin of his fingers was rougher and more exciting than my sister's. He was terribly worked up, and his passion frightened me for a moment or two, but as he fondled me, my own passion took control of me.

"But it was not just his fondling me that excited me so much. It was the feel of his skin against mine. Somehow, I was so worked up that all my inhibitions disappeared. I had always wondered what I would do when I came face to face with the situation when I would have to see or touch a real live penis. Now, confronted with the moment of truth, there was no hesitation.

"I began to undo the buttons of his flies. It was not easy, and he helped me, and when they were undone, he wriggled his way out of his shorts. The bulge in his Y-fronts made me hesitate, but in the hair covering his belly the exposed head of his penis nestled like a bird in its nest. It intrigued me, and kneeling astride him, I put both hands on the band of his Y-fronts and pulled them down. (Remember, this was the first time I had had a sexual experience with a man.)

"I think I must have gasped, because he said, 'What's the matter?' I didn't reply. I was totally unprepared for the sight of this creature, which, as

I looked at it, every now and again, twitched and throbbed.

"He reached up his hands and put them on my breasts. His touch unsettled me still more, and getting off him, I lay down beside him, unable to take my eyes from his thing. My sex felt swollen as it had never felt before, and I was so wet I was certain I must be marking the cover on the bed. I wanted to touch that thing that seemed to have its own source of life, and presently I plucked up courage and did so. I was surprised by the rich silkiness of the skin, and the way the skin moved over whatever it was that it covered; and I was intrigued by the formation of the head.

"Then I heard myself saying as though to myself, 'He's beautiful, beautiful!' Kit grinned and said, 'I'm glad you like him, because he thinks you're beautiful, too.'

"He began to kiss me all over, with his hand between my legs doing indescribable things to my clitoris. The whole of my sex was throbbing and every now and again a muscle somewhere down there tightened and relaxed. Presently I could stand it no longer, I wanted him to come in me. But I didn't know how to tell him, so I took hold of his thing again and pulled it towards me, and thank God, he knew what I meant.

"Only as he placed himself on top of me did I remember. 'It's my first time,' I whispered, 'be gentle.' He put his mouth on mine, and after a little search, his thing found where to go, and he went in very slowly, and I could feel him filling me completely. But there was no pain.

" 'Am I hurting?' Kit asked. 'I didn't feel anything. Not a twinge,' I told him. 'Thank God for gym,' he grinned. 'Who's Jim?' I asked. He laughed, and I felt his thing jump inside me, as if it was also enjoying the joke.

"Kit snuggled his head against mine and whispered in my ear, 'Oh, this is so good, so good.' He tickled behind my ear with the tip of his tongue, and shivers ran all over my body and down to my thing, and made me gasp. Automatically, I thrust myself against him, and he began to move inside me. I thought I was going to die. In seconds it burst all over me and I cried out. I couldn't help it, it was so overwhelming. Then he began to pant, and all of a sudden he thrust his thing up inside me and stayed still, while his thing gave great throbs, possibly seven or eight, and I could feel his heart thumping against mine. When the throbs stopped, he moved again, lowering himself right down on me, his whole body relaxed. He kept whispering, 'Darling, darling, darling!' and all I could do was to stroke his hair, and run my hands over his back and bottom.

"In a few minutes, I felt his thing slip out of me, and Kit rolled over and lay beside me. I wanted to give his thing a thank-you kiss, but when I moved to do so, I couldn't believe what I saw. That little, shrunken, wrinkled, soft, timid thing, no longer full of its own importance and I just couldn't kiss it.

"That was four years ago. Since then I suppose I've made love two or three hundred times, more than half of them with Kit, and the rest with three other boys. Not since have I been really turned on until I've been able to see their erections. The sight of the limp penis leaves me cold. To me it is the most sexless thing in the world. But the moment it begins to swell and stand up, I'm away and there is no holding me back." (British, aged twenty-two, single.)

* * * *

"I don't know why they don't have striptease for women. I've heard it said that it's because women don't react visually to the male naked body as men do to the female naked body. But I just don't believe it. I've always found that a man's naked body, provided he isn't paunchy or flabby, is even more beautiful than a woman's, and I've never yet seen a naked man who didn't move gracefully, even if he was awkward when dressed. I suppose a naked man standing still doesn't turn me on, even when he's facing me. But when he moves I go hot and cold all over. It's not just the swaying of his cock that does it, though I must admit that a naked man with an erection coming towards me with his cock slapping against his belly almost makes me climax, but the movements of the muscles under the skin, especially in the thighs and back, and most of all the quivering of his buttocks. Jack, my husband, knows how I get turned on when he comes from the bathroom with an erection, and he often does it on purpose. He comes towards the bed, or the dressing table, very slowly, making his cock slap loudly against his belly. Neither of us says a word, and there's no foreplay. If I'm on the bed, he just mounts me, and if I'm at the dressing table he lifts me up and comes in me from behind. Either way I come as soon as he's in, and I may come two or three times more, if he doesn't come off quickly himself. Sometimes when we're standing up, he smacks one of his buttocks, and when I hear it, it's just like the sound his cock makes against his belly. When he does that, I always have multi-orgasms. Sometimes we do it from behind, standing up, in front of a mirror so that we can both see his cock going in and out. This is extremely exciting for both of us. When we do it Jack nearly always comes off twice without losing his erection, while I lose count. Once Jack came off three times, and said he could have again, but I'd climaxed so often I felt so weak I couldn't stand any longer.

"But to get back to striptease for women. Not long after we married Jack and I went to a party, and later on it began to get a little bit wild. There were two young boy dancers there. Someone said they were gay and lived together, but they didn't look gay to me. Anyhow, someone put Ravel's *Bolero* on the record player, and the boys began to dance to it, making it up as they went along. It was hot in the room, though all the windows were open and it was November, and the sweat began to pour off them. First one, then the other, unbuttoned his shirt and tore it off. Then they began to undo their trousers, slowly pulling the zips down inch by inch, and then suddenly let them drop. All the women shrieked and clapped, and I noticed most of the men looked a bit sheepish, but that didn't last long when they saw how excited the women were getting.

"The boys slipped out of their trousers. They were dancing barefoot, and their trousers were those wide bell-bottomed ones you can buy in the King's Road, so they didn't have any difficulty. They were both wearing those continental very brief, see-through briefs, and that made the women more excited than ever.

"You know how the *Bolero* works up to a loud crescendo and how the rhythm gets more and more exciting. I don't think the boys were aware of us others at all, they were dancing just for themselves. Watching them, it was the first time I realised how exciting the movements of muscles are. They were so turned on by the erotic music that before long, they began to get erections, and the harder their cocks got, the more they strained against their briefs. I think one of them must have been in pain, because he tried to slip his hand inside his briefs while he was still dancing and move his cock upright. But the briefs were too tight, and all of a sudden, he ripped off his briefs, just tore them off. And the other did the same.

"There was a sudden silence then, except for the music. I have never seen anything quite so beautiful, except the ballet in *Oh! Calcutta!* which also turned me on tremendously. I was actually on the verge of coming during the last part. I think if

Jack had just touched me on my bottom I believe I would have.

"When the music stopped, the two boys rushed out of the room to tremendous applause. They came back a few minutes later, without their erections (Jack says they'd had to go to the bathroom to bring themselves off, they were so worked up). Then our host butted in with their trousers and shirts, and they put them on, and gradually the party quietened down a little, but not much. Part of it may have been due to the music, which is a very erotic piece, isn't it? But I'm sure most of it was due to the dance. I spoke to several of my friends afterwards, and they all said how exciting it had been, and how they could see it again. This I do know, it opened up a new experience for me, and Jack has been wise enough to make use of it. But then he is wise, as well as loving. No, don't tell me women don't react to naked men!"

(British, twenty-six and married, one child and another on the way.)

iii. Paintings, Photographs, Statues

"Look, there aren't, well, 'girlie' magazines—I mean showing male nudes—for women, because women just aren't turned on by looking at pictures, photographs or statues of male nudes, whether they are just simply erotic or pornographic."

That, or something very like it, has been said over and over again to me ever since I began to display an interest in these matters. It is a widely held view, and one which Kinsey supported:

> Something more than half (54 per cent) of the males in our sample had been erotically aroused by seeing photographs or drawings or paintings of nude females, just as they were aroused upon observing living females. . . . Fewer (12 per cent) of the females in the sample had ever been aroused by seeing photographs or drawings or paintings of either male or female nudes. . . .
> [Which means that 88 per cent had NEVER been so aroused—R.C.]
> Photographs of female nudes and magazines exhibiting nude or near nude females are produced primarily for the consumption of males. There are, however, photographs and magazines portraying nude and near nude males—but these are also produced for the consumption of males. There are almost no male or female nudes which are produced for the consumption of females. *The failure of nearly all females to find erotic arousal in such photographs is so well known to distributors of nude photographs and nude magazines that they have considered that it would not be financially profitable to produce such material for a primarily female audience.* [My italics—R.C.] *

Is this still the situation, or have women changed since Kinsey published his survey in 1953, just twenty years ago? What do women say?

Of our 198 women, 108 (approximately 55 percent) do react sexually to pictorial representations of the male nude. Of the 108, 76 are turned on by any material that appeals to them (which is also the male's reaction, as it is to his observing living

* Kinsey, *Sexual Behavior in the Human Female*, pp. 652–3.

females), while the remaining 32 are only aroused by specific objects or of photographs, pictures, or statues of males who remind them of their actual lovers or of their male "sexy" ideal. As with males and representations of female nudes, many of our women use this kind of material as an accompaniment to masturbation. Not all women are turned on by all three—pictures, photographs, statues—but respond to one or two, or if they do respond to all three it is in varying degrees.*

Let's see what some of the women say, who respond specifically.

Marion, twenty-seven, British, single, living in London, England, writes, "Pictures and photographs that match my No. 1 arouse me without fail, and so does Michelangelo's statue of David, though David isn't my ideal sexy type."

Amanda, twenty-two, married, living in Charleston, West Virginia:

"I have many nude photographs of Tom which I took in the garden of a house we once rented for a holiday. It was a fantastically romantic garden and quite secluded. When he is away from home, I get out these photographs and always end up by bringing myself off, they make me so horny."

Phyllis, twenty-four, single, black, living in Cambridge, Massachusetts:

"Pictures and paintings which are abstract and subtle in which I can read implications of phallic

---

* These figures tend to show that there has been a change in women in this area of sexual response over the last twenty years. I shall be referring to this change—and others—in my final chapter.

symbols or nudity or anything that reminds me of sensuality involved in sex with my number one man."

Linda, twenty-six, single but has a permanent relationship, British, lives in Oxford, England:

"I have only been turned on by one picture, I think because the magazine and other pictures would have to be ultraerotic to have any effect on me. I saw this picture one night in a street in Soho. I was being shown round London by a very close friend (a very puritanical one) when a man appeared in a white coat and hat from the front of a cafe, and quickly selected some cheaply framed oil paintings from a pile leaning up against the cafe wall. I only saw one, the most beautiful thing I have ever seen. It was a side view of a naked man (my 'ideal' actually) with a strong erection. His penis was circumcised, with a slight upward curve. I can still see it and the memory gets me swollen and moist even now. If I hadn't been dragged away so quickly, I would have bought it, then and there. The cover of one of the earlier *Forum*s had a similar effect. I'm afraid I can't remember which one, as I always give them away. It was a black and white drawing of a girl and two young men.

"As for statues, now and then one of an unveiled female figure can make me aware of my sex-lips and nipples. I possess one at the moment, one I brought back from Greece, a small slim Grecian girl with small round breasts, neat waist, and curving tummy. I often look at it when I'm playing with myself, and generally have a more intense climax than when I fantasise about Bill. (I hope that doesn't mean I'm 'kinky'?)"

A number of women, who claim to be exclusively heterosexual, have referred to similar arousal by pictures or photographs of other women, sometimes when they are accompanied by a man. I don't consider such reactions kinky; they merely indicate, I suggest, a tendency toward bisexuality which is not to be feared, but rather joyfully accepted, since the bisexual has the best of both sexual worlds.

Of the women who responded more generally, Jeanne, twenty-seven, the New York airline stewardess, says, "I like good pictures of the human body, either male or female, and am quite aroused by them. I saw a statue of a penis in a temple in India, and was really turned on by it. I've thought of it many times. I also saw in India the temples of Khajuraho which contain fantastic erotic carvings. The figures are so blatantly erotic, the imagination of the sculptor so vivid! We took many photographs. I look at them frequently."

Susi, twenty-four and married, has two children and lives in Miami, Florida. She says, "I have heard that the female is *not* supposed to be aroused by pictures etc., but I am. Photos of a well-built nude male with a large limp cock—a large limp cock has more effect on me than an erect one, unless it's like a stallion's—always gets me horny. I know *Forum* says you can't tell from the limp cock's size how much bigger it will be when hard, but I imagine to myself that it will be very big, and I'm ready to take it in no time. Apart from this, I'm not turned on by any one thing or object."

Francesca, aged thirty and divorced ten years, lives in Colchester, England. She is sexually roused by pictures and photographs, but not by statues. "Pictures of nude or nearly nude women, especially if they are in some lesbian pose, or being spanked or moderately roughly handled by a man, hot me up in no time." She, too, claims to be exclusively heterosexual.

Dawn, thirty and divorced, living in Chicago, gives interesting reasons for her sexual reaction to pictures. "Occasionally a picture of a man who looks 'sexy' will rouse me sexually, and paintings of sensual and opulent and even decadent settings occasionally rouse me, too, because these are the settings in which my sexual fantasies are set. Photographs of such settings are not so good because they lack the 'life' there is in a painting. Occasionally statues of nude male figures rouse me if they look strong—not muscular, but strong."

Caroline is another American, forty-six, and lives in Rochester, New York. "This year I got myself a calendar that has photographs of nude men. The photographs are tastefully done, and most of the men fit my description of a sexy man. Some of the photographs in the calendar rouse me to the extent of erecting my clit and nipples and making my vulva swell. The picture for June, which shows a man and his young son together makes this happen in seconds."

Can one continue to insist that women are difficult

to arouse sexually? Or is Kinsey right when he says that women are only slow to arouse when they are in a sexual situation with a man? It looks like it, though there are signs that many are quickly changing in these respects.

"The only sort of pictures that have an effect on me," says Emma, twenty-four, English, and single, "are some of the male models in underwear, e.g., pants, vests, or socks."

Lynne, the twenty-six-year-old, single American, who is attracted by men's naked bottoms, is—may I say, naturally?—aroused by some statues of nude males. "There is one statue in particular at the National Gallery of Fine Art in Washington, D.C., that I really like. It is a slightly smaller than life-size statue of a nude male. I especially like the way it looks from behind. It has a perfect bottom, and I can hardly resist putting my hand on its bottom and feeling it. In addition, the body build of this statue is very close to the build I find most attractive to me. Also, its genitals are perfectly formed, and its penis is uncircumcised. I prefer statues of nude males over photographs or paintings of them. When it comes to paintings or photos, I sometimes become aroused by those showing nude females in idyllic outdoor settings. I like to imagine myself as one of the women in such a painting or photo."

Rodin's sculpture, *The Kiss*, figures in many of the replies. This is not surprising, granted one accepts that women are sexually aroused by statues, since *The Kiss* is one of the most well-known of art in the Western world.

Anita, an American college student, expresses the views of many. "Any good erotic nude male stuff turns me on, if it is done with taste and intelligence. The crude stuff bores me, particularly like copulation depicted. But a masturbating man or woman certainly burns me up. Would like to have a collection of very fine erotic art."

Audrey, another American, twenty-three, married, is aroused by pictures and photographs of "the actions portrayed just before intercourse. In statues the nude body of a relaxed male turns me on, but what turns me on most is a picture of an erect penis or of a panting, feverishly hot woman."

That she is roused by the nude body of a relaxed male is a little strange, because she is unaffected by observing a limp penis.

Marianne is twenty-nine, married with two children, and lives in Derby, England. She presents a very interesting case, as we shall see.

"When we first began watching 'blue' films, they were very, very crude, and I wasn't turned on at all. In fact, quite the reverse. I think it was because the setting was always so sleazy and the actors weren't at all beautiful or good-looking, and they really didn't seem to know much about making love. I think one of the things that put me off most of all was the men's penises, most of which looked grotesque. The thought of letting some of these organs come anywhere near me, let alone come in me, or caressing them or going down on them made me feel physically sick.

"Then one of our friends got a batch of really well made German films. They were in colour, and trouble had been taken over the production. The sets (they looked like real rooms) were, what shall I say?—opulent, and the actors were young, lovely to look at, clean and wholesome looking, and they certainly knew what it was all about. Richard and I, who consider ourselves quite sophisticated lovers (we do everything you talk about in your book *The Sensuous Couple*, and one or two things of our own, which we will tell you about one day, if you would like to hear) well, we learned one or two quite exciting tips from them. They had also gone to the trouble of having a story. It wasn't a very strong plot, but it made the sex parts all the more natural, because they weren't naked or in sexual situations all the time. For the first time in my life, I got really turned on, and the others said the same. And I'm sure it's true, because the party we had after the showing was much more, well, exciting. I mean, it was obvious that everyone was terrifically turned on, and it went on for much longer than usual. At parties I generally like to stay with Richard. I don't mind if he goes with someone else or gets involved in a group, but though I like our male friends as friends, I don't feel attracted to any of them sexually, except perhaps one, and I've never had it off with him. When Richard wanders, I go out to the kitchen and make coffee. Well, this time it wasn't like that at all. Before I really realised what was happening, Richard and I were part of a group, and soon I'd lost count of all the climaxes I'd had and was having. (Usually I have two or three, rarely more.) At least three men came with me that night, and there was one time when three men were making love to me at the same time, which I had never thought I would care for, and so had avoided, but I must say, it was absolutely fantastic. Mind you, I think I was lucky in my partners. They'd obviously been in this situation before, and knew exactly what they were doing.

"But after we had looked at these films half a dozen times, they began to pall. Good as they were, they didn't turn us on any more. I suppose this is natural, in a way. You can have too much of a good thing, whatever it is, except sex, but even then you've got to keep ringing the changes to stop you from being bored.

"The day after the first time we'd seen these films, Eileen, whose husband had got them, rang me up and said there was one film Grant hadn't screened at the party. Would I like to see it? Madge and Emmy wanted to, and she thought I might like to. I asked her what was so special about it, but she wouldn't tell me. 'Wait and see,' she said, 'but I'm sure it will interest you, if nothing else.' Well, as you can imagine, that made me curious, and I said yes, I would join them. So she said come over to lunch, and we'll look at it before we have to go pick up the children from school.

"While we were having lunch, we kept asking Eileen what was so special about the film, but she wouldn't tell us. Wait and see, she said. But when she was adjusting the projector she said Grant didn't know how this film had got mixed up with his, because he certainly hadn't chosen it, and he hadn't paid for it. As you can guess, we were all very curious at all this mystery.

"However, as soon as the film began to roll, it was all revealed. It began with a handsome boy of about twenty looking in a shop window at some motor bicycles. Presently another handsome boy comes along and stops and looks and they speak to one another. They are obviously motorcycling enthusiasts and are discussing the merits of the various models.

"After a minute or two, they walk off, still talking animatedly. Next you see them outside a block of flats, and the first one is inviting the other up to his flat. It's really a bed-sitter, simply but elegantly furnished. The host gets some beer, switches on the record player, and then shows the guest some motorcycling magazines. The host lolls on the bed while the guest sits on a chair near him, looking at the magazines, discussing some point or other about a particular machine.

"When they've gone through the magazines, they sit chatting and drinking their beer. They are both wearing tight trousers and turtlenecked pullovers and boots. Presently you become aware from the bulge in his trousers that the guest is getting sexually aroused. I don't know how they did it with the cameras and the crew and the producer there, but the camera just showed the guest's crotch and held it, and you could see his penis swelling and hardening under his trousers. We were all four of us turned on by that. It looked as if his erection was causing him some discomfort, because he put his hand on the bulge and squeezed it.

"I won't give the rest of the film in detail, but I'm being absolutely honest when I say that it was one of the best 'blue' films I've ever seen. The two boys were so obviously very fond of one another. In fact, if the film-story hadn't made them meet by chance, so that they didn't really have long enough to fall in love, I would have said they were really in love. Perhaps they were in real life, because I doubt whether they could have acted it so beautifully as they did.

"I had always wondered what gay men did with one another when they made love. I thought that because there was a vital organ missing, it must be unsatisfactory whatever they did, and that all the foreplay, because of this, must be wasted effort. But these two boys made it seem so natural and right, even when they took it in turns to go into one another. You see, they used the position a straight couple can use, and when you couldn't see the passive one's penis, you would have thought he was a woman, and as you only had an occasional glimpse of it, it was, what shall I say, well, convincing. They really knew how to make love, too. Richard always says that no other woman has ever gone down on him like me, but there was a long scene in close-up of the host doing fellatio, and he did things that had never occurred to me, though it's one of the best things I like doing.

"When it was finished I realised how turned on I was, and all the others were the same. But if anyone tells you that women *don't* get turned on by films of men, don't believe them."

(By the way, they persuaded Grant to show the film at the next party, and all the women admitted to being much aroused by it, while only two of the men claimed to be turned off by it.)

I said earlier that this is a very interesting case, and this is why. It is very well-known that a large number of men are highly sexually roused by watching women making lesbian love. (This is the motive behind most husbands' requests that they and their wives practice troilism, stipulating that the third partner be a woman.) The Danes were quick to exploit this by invariably beginning their "live shows" with a lesbian act. I have spoken to many women who have watched such acts, and while a few, who have later turned out to be bisexuals, have admitted to being roused in varying degrees, the majority are not. Until now, I have never heard it suggested that women would react in the same way to a male gay scene.

As I shall be explaining later, we are most of us, men and women, voyeurs, but men more so than women. I have been told by women who have participated in group sex that they are less interested in the sexual activities of those around them with whom they are not involved, than they are in seeing how their partners are making out. Men, however, affirm just the opposite. It is, nevertheless, a fact that once a group scene has got into swing, the women do respond to its visual stimulation to a not much lesser degree than men. This female response to visual stimulation is confirmed by the fact that almost as many women as men are aroused, when making love in private with their partners, by adopting such a position for coupling which will allow them to watch in a mirror the penis sliding in and out of the vagina.

The psychiatrists explain the male penchant for watching lesbian lovemaking by maintaining that they are able to experience sexual arousal without being sexually involved with women. This seems to me to suggest a male fear of sexual involvement with women on a scale which must be almost universal. Of course, there are a number of men who while having a sexual relationship with women do so reluctantly, and do have a conscious or unconscious sexual fear of them—a fear of symbolic castration, of deprivement of virility, of a sapping of their manhood. I personally find it quite impossible to accept this thesis as applied to the vast numbers of men who are sexually roused by watching lesbian acts; for if it were true, then it would follow that the majority of men have a sexual fear of women. If that were so, then the timeless image of the male as hunter and sexual seducer of the female is a fallacy of the very first order. It would also mean that our entire sexual relationship is a depraved one, since we would be going against Nature by doing something Nature does not want us to do. This is palpably false, or else we have been deceiving ourselves since time began, by assuring ourselves that our sexual instinct is as strong as our instinct to eat and sleep, and must be equally satisfied.

In my view, it is our tendency to bisexuality, or our actual bisexuality, which is responsible for the male's capability to be roused by lesbian lovemaking. (I have said elsewhere that the more I study human sexual nature, the more convinced I become that bisexuality is the norm, and exclusive heterosexuality and exclusive homosexuality are the deviations.) In addition to this bisexuality factor, there is the male's easy response to visual stimuli.

With the evidence with which my collaborators have supplied me in this study, I feel certain we shall be able to say that what applies to men in this respect, applies also to women.

Gilly is twenty-five, unmarried, but lives with her future husband at Chelmsford, England, about thirty miles from London. They are sharing a flat in a block from which children are excluded, and are saving up for a deposit on a house. When they have bought a house they will marry. Though every penny counts, wisely they have a night out in London once a month.

"Roger was very keen to see *Oh! Calcutta!* I had misgivings, because I thought I might be embarrassed. You see, Roger is the first man I've ever made love with, and the only man I've ever seen naked. Anyhow, I let myself be persuaded because he was so keen.

"I was very nervous until the curtain went up,

but I found the opening number, 'Taking Off the Robe,' so amusing and the cast so unselfconscious, that I wasn't nervous for long, and I was only embarrassed, and then not much, by the masturbation sketch. Long before the end of the first act, I was feeling terribly randy, not because of the women, but by the sight of all those penises, each of which was different, yet attractive in its own way. But what really turned me on, in fact I climaxed near the end of it, was that beautiful ballet number. That is the most erotic thing I have ever seen."

Isobel lives in Manhattan. She is twenty-one, is not married, but has a regular relationship with her boyfriend, though they do not live together. They will marry when he gets the promotion they are expecting. They join the group-sex scene every six weeks to two months, and consider themselves sexually liberated and sophisticated.

"We went to *Oh! Calcutta!* and our response to it was unbelievable. We went back to my apartment straight afterwards and couldn't wait to take our clothes off. We had it off in the lobby standing up. Then I made some coffee and we went to bed, taking the coffee with us. But we never did get to drinking that coffee. By the time we got around to it, it was stone cold, and neither of us wanted to spoil the lovely state we were in by getting up to heat it up. I lost count of the orgasms I had. Jo had six, not counting the one in the lobby, three of them without coming out of me, and with the same hard-on. We were among the first to see *Deep*

Throat. That turned us on, too, but nothing like *Oh! Calcutta!* What turned me on most was Linda Lovelace's sword-swallowing act. Funnily enough, though, I was aware some time before the end of the film that it was losing its effectiveness a little more each time. Jo agreed. We've seen *Oh! Calcutta!* four times, and every time it's made us as randy as it did the first time. I wouldn't want to see *Deep Throat* again. Jo did go a second time with a man friend, but he said it left him cold."

Brenda is twenty-three, and is married to an airline pilot, consequently she spends some time on her own. They live in Pennington, New Jersey. They have joined Ellen Peck's National Organization for Non-Parents.

"I have pretty strong views on not having sex outside of marriage, so when Paul isn't around, I masturbate when I'm feeling randy. I always feel very randy two or three days before my periods begin, very much more randy than at other times, and do you know what I do? I have this photograph which I cut from a number of *Paris Match*. It's of the beach at San Tropez, and everyone in it is naked. But in the foreground there's this man. I believe he's ——, the film star, but I'm not sure. He hasn't got an erection, of course, but just looking at his beautiful, beautiful body at any time, gets me all steamed up. Well, when I feel extra randy, like I said, I get out this photograph and look at it while I bring myself off, and I always have a blowout. I can't begin to describe it. Do you think I'm kinky, because women aren't supposed to respond to pictures of men, are they?"

Betty, the sixteen-year-old American high-school girl has "some pictures of rock magazines and guys like that, that turn me on. I have a few that show them naked. They were hard for me to get and I have to hide them from my parents. It turns me on most to see the parts of their bodies that are covered by clothes in other pictures. I look at them when I play with myself."

One of the most interesting points regarding this group of responses is the similarity of the material that arouses men with that which arouses women. It emerges, by and large, that what the female breasts are to the male as an arousal factor in visual stimulation the penis is to the female. This applies not only to the living body, but to pictorial material as an aid to psychological stimulation during masturbation. I have a feeling that with the woman's recognition that she has a sexuality which she is prepared to encourage to develop, we shall find that in essence her sexual response is much closer to the male's than we have previously been led to believe.

iv. Other Male Qualities that Turn a Woman On

I have been in somewhat of a quandary about where to place this section. My question was, "If a man's appearance does *not* turn you on, what other male qualities do?" However, a large number of women who were sexually aroused by the male's physical appearance answered this question too, claiming that although they were primarily turned on by physical appearance, they could also be primarily turned on by other qualities, or they needed other qualities in a man before they could be turned on by his appearance, or they needed a combination of qualities in order to be turned on at all.

When I asked my question, I did so on the assumption that if the woman was not visually roused she relied on psychological stimuli to arouse her, and that all the "other qualities" would be psychological. This being so, it would be logical for me to include this section in the next chapter. But it is not so cut-and-dried as I imagined it would be, and after some thought I have decided to include it here.

Sixty-eight women out of the 198 did *not* answer the question. For my male readers, however, I will give a selection of the other 130 women's preferences, so that they may know that they can't hope to make their way between (most) women's legs simply by waving their cocks about.

Susi, the married English girl, put this point well. "The way he comes on. I hate *pushy men*. I like the men who let me know they want me, but yet don't push anything unless I give them some indication I want them to."

Doreen, the English girl who regards sex as "the best thing since sliced bread," put it even better.

"The subtle blend of power and gentleness. The

guy who has an erection and hits you over the head with it makes me almost cold and angry. The guy who wants you badly but is controlling it until it's killing him in order to oh-so-gently arouse you, will have me melting."

Most women want more than crude sexual satisfaction, as do most men, once they've established a regular relationship and have worked through the physical phase. It is this that adds to my oft-repeated contention that if you want to get the most out of sex, you must use physical lovemaking to express the emotional love (respect, affection) you have for one another. My male readers need not be apprehensive; the qualities most women demand are well within the scope of the man who has any self-respect, though there are a few that are distinctive to one or two women.

For example, Charlotte of London, England—"A man's appearance does not necessarily arouse me sexually, although I find a sensual mouth extremely sexy. But I will really go for him if he has a good sense of humour and a good male smell."

(I don't know how one acquires a good male smell. You had better ask your partner.)

Many women have the same requirements as Chrissy of Boston, Massachusetts, who at eighteen says she is "fairly well sexually educated and experienced." She says, "I guess the kiss fits in here. I hate slobbering, preferring gentle sucking. *I like to be appreciated and have this demonstrated. I like to be held and kissed and touched and smiled at often. These all rouse me tremendously*." [Italics mine—R.C.]

Nancy, twenty-nine, who lives in Georgetown, Washington, D.C., has much the same ideas. "Appearance is certainly part of the attraction; however, a gentle, warm and patient male has a great chance of turning me on, even if he's not my 'sexy' type."

Iris, the Toronto call girl, has similar requirements. "Bill has all of the other qualities I find appealing. He is gentle, game for anything, unafraid to express love verbally as well as physically, he is clean and unselfish. He is understanding and strong but sensitive. He is without doubt a highly skilled lover."

Phyllis, the black girl from Washington, D.C., requires her lover to be "obviously intelligent, and intensely interested in his career, regardless of what it is," but Marion of London, England, is more easily satisfied. She says briefly, "He must have a good accent."

Linda, of Oxford, England, is sure that there is often a chemical attraction which is irresistible. "Sometimes," she says, "a man can pass me, or sit next to me in a bus, he can be eighteen or forty-eight, but something passes between us, and this tends to be mutual, as I've discovered when very occasionally I've met them again and asked. Even if I look up and find the man's appearance would be normally repulsive to me, the feeling still lasts—a tightness in my chest and feelings of general sexual excitement. I believe this is a chemical attraction, or it may be 'smell.' If it is, I am not aware of it."

Many other women want what Georgie of San

Francisco wants. "Courteousness, kindness to animals, openmindedness, sure of his sexuality, one who admits his faults, and who can stimulate my mind to fantasy."

Jeanne, the American airline stewardess, after describing at length her ideal male physical standards says, "Physical appearance is really very unimportant to me. I would certainly never sleep with a man because of his looks. I like men I can talk to, I can find men who want to share much of themselves with me, and who enjoy having me do the same. It is with these men—and only with these—that I share sex."

Anita, the American college student, wants "vivacity, warmth and kindness (warmth and kindness turn me on like nothing else), highly intelligent, good conversationalist, good sense of humor, amiability, love of having a good time."

Margaret, of Cambridge, England, likes her man to be "mildly arrogant and aggressive, thoughtful and gentle—like father."

Joanne, an English girl of twenty-four, claims that "appearance does matter initially, but of course I can love a man once I know him, even though he is not good-looking. But he must be gentle, firm, and tactful."

Jeanette, twenty-two, married, living in Wilmington, North Carolina, is most turned on by a strong, masculine voice, so long as "he is capable of being tender and gentle when needed." Susan, nineteen, American, has already discovered a few home truths. "One male quality that turns me on is the way a man shows he really cares. I like when he builds me up before having intercourse. *Some* men just don't really care about the woman, they only care about their erection and orgasm."

Women want to be shown consideration, and so they should.

Edith, who lives in Scotland, likes "meeting a man for the first time, having extra pressure in the handshake, accompanied by a lingering, meaningful look. A man who removes my coat as if he were removing my dress. A man who dances with me as if I were an extension of his body."

Marilyn, from Richmond, Virginia, who finds that "the physical appearance is not the 'thing' that turns me on, but the manner in which a man reacts to me as an individual," wants her ideal "sexy" man to have—

(a) Penetrating and "interested" eyes.
(b) The ability to make a woman feel she is something special.
(c) Gentleness and tenderness, which, incidentally, does not emasculate him in the average woman's eyes.
(d) A slightly mysterious quality.

Cassandra, from San Diego, California, who is deeply in love with her partner, is more embracing in her requirements, which, happily, she has found in her lover.

"His *passion*, not *just* for lovemaking but about everything he *cares* about—politics, his family, his job, me, whatever. His personal honor, pride, integrity. (How can two people carry on an extramarital affair and have those qualities?) We can and do, and he does have them. We have met some humiliating experiences and dangers as a result of our loving each other, but I'm proud of his reactions and responses. A fine, brave man."

Is Peggy, of Chicago, Illinois, wanting much the same thing? She is twenty-nine, and claims to be a liberated woman. " 'Love' is not essential to my screwing a man. I feel affection and desire is all that is necessary. I am not frigid, though I do not climax every time by all means. This depends on my mood and current man." But can she be as "liberated" as she thinks? She goes on, "A man's 'manliness' is a sure-fire way to rouse me. I like a man who exudes an aura of self-confidence and masculinity (not conceit or brutality). *I like a man who takes charge and is somewhat domineering.* [Italics mine—R.C.] Can't stand prissy, delicate, gentle types who defer constantly to my wishes."

Marie of Torrance, California, says, "I like my partner to let me know that he's really freaking out as a result of what I'm doing to him. There are some men who are very accomplished lovers, I mean they know every trick of the trade, they really do, and can turn you on until you're wild for them to come in you. But all the while they're doing they never say a word, and never make a sound, and they come in you and buck away and then suddenly stop and you know they've come, and you'd never know it either from the noise they make, like breathing heavy or groaning, or even showing it on their faces. Even when they say thank you afterwards it's like adding insult to injury. Why do you think this is, Dr. Chartham? Is it because they don't feel anything much, either while they are making love, or when they come off?

"I've read your book *The Sensuous Couple* and what you say in it about making noises (erolalia, you call it) while you're having it off, and I agree with you that it does sort of free you and make every sensation so much bigger and better, especially coming off. Until I read your book I used to whimper a little bit as I was building up to come off, only for a second or two, and it was quite automatic. Then I thought I'd try your advice, and sound off during foreplay whenever something felt a little bit nicer than usual, and then as I got more randy, to make more and more noise, until I came off with a kind of shriek. Boy, the first time I did it, when I came off I nearly blew my mind. I'd never had a climax like it. So after that I sort of trained myself to make all sorts of noises, and when I compare what I feel now with what I used to feel, it's unbelievable that just doing that makes such a difference to what you feel physically. Now I can do it automatically without thinking about it. My partners like it too. I think they think they're real Casanovas, making me act this way, and I don't mind them thinking that, because it does make them better than they would usually be.

"But to get back to liking my partners to show some appreciation. I suppose, in fact I know, it works on me exactly the same as it does with them. Before I started letting myself go noisewise, if my partner was one of these really silent types, I never had an orgasm, whatever he tried to do to me afterwards. I remember one guy was so turned off by my noises that he just couldn't come, though he fucked me for what seemed eternity, with me coming off I don't know how often. In the end, he said, 'Look, Marie, do you mind being quiet, just as I'm coming you make one of those fucking sounds of yours, and it puts me off. Just lie still and quiet, there's a good baby.' So I lay quiet and still, and ten more thrusts and he had shot his load, but I wouldn't have known it if I hadn't felt his cock jerking a little bit, and his rather grim 'Thank God,' as he rolled off me. 'Christ!' he said, 'I thought I was never going to come. Do you always make a ruckus like that?' 'Yes,' I told him. 'Well, don't do it again when you're with me, there's a good chick.' 'Look,' I told him, 'if you don't like it, find another chick.' I never saw him again.

"My present boy friend, who I'm going to marry at Easter, is just the opposite. He likes me to make love to him while he just lies there and does nothing except tickle my clit if it should happen to come within reach. I think he would like it this way every time, but that would make him lazy, I guess, and anyway, though I don't mind being active, in fact, it gives me quite a kick, I like a change every now and again. But when he's particularly in this mood to do nothing but just lie there and let me do anything to him I can think of, I never refuse him, because I know he's going to be more appreciative than ordinary, and will come nearer to blowing his mind, which always makes me nearly blow mine.

"I've had quite a lot of experience with men, as I'm sure you'll have guessed by this time, but not one of them has been so sensitive as Gary. The whole of his skin is a sensitive zone. It doesn't matter where you touch him, he responds. And how he responds! There are two or three spots more sensitive than others, just inside the opening in his cock, just above the bottom of his cock on the underside, and a special spot on his right thigh about level with his balls.

"Heavy caresses don't do anything to him at all, but the lighter you can run your finger tips or your tongue over him, the wilder he responds. He writhes and squirms, throws back his head and bares his teeth, and his cock sometimes jumps out of my hand, and all the time he's moaning and saying 'Christ, Marie,' though usually it's a long drawn-out 'No . . o . . o, no . . o . . o!' When we were having it off like this the first time, and he said 'No,' I stopped what I was doing because I thought he didn't like it. 'Why have you stopped?' he said. 'You said "no" so I thought I was hurting you.' Then he explained that when he said 'No . . o . . o' like that it was being specially good. 'Then why don't you say "yes," or "that's good," I said. 'You can't say "yes" or "that's good" with your teeth clenched,' he said, 'and when I clench my teeth it makes it even better.' I didn't really believe it, but when I tried it the next time he was doing me, he was right. I'm not clever enough to explain why or what happens when you clench your teeth, but you try it, Dr. Chartham.

"Well as I say, he's noisy and he's never still, and when he comes you think there's an earthquake. When I've been doing him, I usually end up with me kneeling astride him, which is a position I really dig. Just as the first spurt is coming, he throws back his head and rolls it from side to side, and says "No" at the top of his voice, and arches his back so much that I'm sure I could crawl under him. The first time this happened he took me by surprise so much that he threw me right off his cock, and I couldn't get back in again until he'd finished spurting. It happened again the second time, but now I've learned to read the signs, and ride him like a steer. You can guess the effect all this has on me. It makes me feel really great, because I'm doing this to him. I'm making him cry out, and squirm and roll about, and it's his showing his appreciation in this way that turns me on, and I come at the slightest touch, and sometimes without being touched at all, and it's always a bomb when I come off.

"I'm afraid I've gone on rather a lot, Dr. Chartham, but you did ask for the fullest details. Anyway, I hope it helps your study, and if nothing else you know why I'm going to marry Gary."

Lastly, I cannot resist Jan, the girl of the seventy lovers.

"I guess I should not be answering this question since I answered No. 1, but it logically belongs here. A male quality which arouses me intensely is the intense desire, longing, or burning that guys can experience and communicate to me when they are in need of sex. I know I am expressing this badly.

113

"I believe at the very beginning of a date I can intuit a great deal about the sexual needs of a guy. Some would simply like to have sex with me for the experience, pleasure, and adding a new conquest to their list. This situation does not rouse me, so if I do have sex with him it is because of other factors.

"Others may feel a great need, and they communicate this feeling to me even if they may be shy or afraid of requesting a sexual relationship. This situation rouses me and I prefer it that way. I like the feeling that a guy is burning for me. It gives me a feeling of power and it makes me feel good. Further, I find a boy in that state more grateful and will do anything possible to please me. Some will actually beg for it, and this rouses me.

"I remember a boy at the university just begging to get his hands in my pants. It roused me. I remember a Spanish boy about nineteen, who shared a compartment with me in a train and then a lay-over stop for several hours, waiting for the next train. We took a walk through the town (it was night) and never having had sex before, he begged for the smallest favors. This aroused me fantastically and he was grateful. I had a feeling of great power and I enjoyed sex with him very much.

"In short, even though I really want sex with a boy, I prefer it to appear he wants it with me more than I do with him. The more he burns for it and begs, the more I am roused."

Jan, if you ever read this book, please get in touch with me via the publishers, or *Forum*.

2

It's All in the Mind

···→·━━◆>◆<◆━━·→··

THE EVIDENCE of the previous chapter has shown that as with the male, so with the female, visual stimuli are translated into psychological stimuli; that, in fact, unless there can be this translation of the visual into the psychological there can be no sexual stimulation. Kinsey lumped all the various visual stimuli considered in the last chapter with those I deal with in this chapter under "Psychologic Factors in Sexual Response," and was, of course, right to do so. But I have separated them from purely cerebral stimuli (which we are going to look at now) because I wished to draw attention to the fact that we must now be very wary in alleging, as has long been alleged, that the average woman does not respond to visual stimuli as often or as immediately at does the average male.

In this chapter we are going to look at the effect of erotic stimulants that can only be perceived by the brain—the written word, erotic thoughts or fantasies, music, and the oral discussion of sexual matters, including erotic stories told verbally.

Again, it has long been widely held—though not widely supported by Kinsey—that all these types of stimuli, which are sexually arousing to the majority of average males, draw sexual arousal response from very few average women. Considering the large number of *Forum*'s women correspondents who refer to being aroused by the kinds of material I have just listed—this has been especially noticeable over the last three years—it would not surprise me to learn that there have been changes here also.

Let's see what has happened.

i. The Written Word

I differentiate here between hard-core pornography and erotic material. The hard-core porn is the generally badly written, blatantly explicit, and exaggerated accounts of fucking, penis size, and both male and female copulatory capacity. Such stuff as:

> One by one she undid his buttons. She felt a bulge underneath that was raising her in the air. After the fourth button, she tried to slip her hand in, but it was useless. A stiff brownish snake seemed to jump out and knife the atmosphere. She was thrown off Sylvester's lap, and when she lifted herself to her knees she was face to face with the most powerful cock she had ever

seen. It was stiff and solid and stood up like a bed-post. She put her two hands along it; it was five hand-breadths long, and her hand would not go round it.

Sally thought that this one might be her dimensions. And so it was. It fit tight and snug and her cunt was even pushed open a bit wider. But the finest thing was that Sylvester obeyed her, and he never came until she had had her pleasure three or four times. Then he would explode and his fluid would enter and spurt along in powerful jets. He was like a volcano and it was hard to believe that all this thunder could come from such a little man.

(From *The Insatiable Sally* by Louis Clark. This is mild when compared with much hard-core porn. Even this author can do much better, but his "best" bits invariably make me sick to my stomach, and I wanted to save you that.)

There is, however, much erotic material, beauti-fully written, either explicit or suggestive, which has the power of sexually arousing most men. "The Song of Solomon" in the Old Testament *Apoc-rypha* is one of the most erotic works in any lan-guage, and there are passages in D. H. Lawrence (not just *Lady Chatterley*), John Updike, Alexis Lykiard, and Agnar Mykle—to name only a few —that have this power. They are works which you can put on your open bookshelves or your coffee table, and not mind who sees them. This is the ma-terial I have in mind.

A little more than two-thirds of our 198 women admitted to being sexually roused by such material, and their choices are many and varied.

117

" 'The Song of Solomon' is my favorite. Also sex manuals, and *The Intimate Kiss* by Gershon Legman." (American.)

"*The Naked Lunch* by Burroughs, and the words 'manhood' and 'member.' " (American.)

The power of single words, especially the four-letter words, is often amazing. A woman wrote to me once wanting reassurance about a fantasy. She was much aroused sexually by seeing on TV a famous tennis star. She wanted her husband to be like him, then she was sure she would easily achieve the ever elusive orgasm. "Why don't you," I suggested, "imagine that it is X who is making love to you, that it is his *cock* that is up in you? We are often justified in playing such games with ourselves, and if this helps you to come off, then I say you would be justified."

A day or two later, I received a reply. "It worked! But do you know what really did it? It was your use of the word 'cock.' I had always thought of X's organ as his 'penis.' Even when I read your phrase imagine 'it is his cock that's up you,' I was so turned on, I had to masturbate, and I came in about a minute. Usually it takes about ten minutes when I masturbate. During intercourse I never come off at all even if my husband thrusts for half-an-hour and he's played with me for another half-an-hour before going in me. Last night I came in about five minutes after he came up me, and it was very intense. He was so surprised, he couldn't come, and had to give up in the end. But I had another three orgasms, a thing that has never happened to me before. Do you mind my using this rather crude language when I write to you, but it brings me on heat beautifully? I shall masturbate when I've finished this. What is wrong with me?"

Another American writes, "I like poetry. *Leaves of Grass* by Walt Whitman, *This is My Beloved*, and the 'Song of Solomon.' All these make me very horny. (The description of a lover in the 'Song' says everything about whether and how women *are* attracted by the physical appearance of their lover. All people have some attractive features. It's not necessary to be all beautiful.) There are not enough writings by women expressing sexual love, but there are some I read when I can find them. I *write* to my lover about everything. Making love I am inarticulate. I moan and make sounds but not sense, so I *write* to him and tell him all my thoughts, romantic and sexual, using all the old Anglo-Saxon words and describe my fantasies, which we sometimes act out."

Marilyn of Richmond, Virginia, says, "Books and the written word—definitely yes. My imagination is freer and it's easier to relate to characters and situations. Besides, it feels more private."

Edith of Oxford, England, writes:

"Books—yes!

" 'Collogue' type articles in *Mayfair*, *Men Only*, *Penthouse*.

"Certain articles and letters in *Forum* which deal with female arousal and techniques unknown to me.

"*The Sensuous Man*."

Another Englishwoman says, "Written works do

have a powerful effect. My favourite is *Women in Love* by D. H. Lawrence."

"Any well-written erotic book," writes Joanna of Edinburgh, "I find very exciting, e.g., Christie Brown's *Down All the Days*. A short story in *Playboy—Forum* makes me come to the boil in no time just thinking about it. Many of the 'Quest' series in *Mayfair* have the same effect, so do readers' letters in *Forum* and *Penthouse*. Anything that accurately describes lovemaking. The real kind, not the kind that dissolves into dots at the slightest sign of impropriety. All your books do this, especially *The Sensuous Couple*. If we want a really super session, my husband and I read bits of it to one another. Sometimes we act it out, but often we're both so turned on, all we want to do is fuck and come. Then after a time we read a bit more, and take things more slowly."

Our other American college student, Anita, responds to "most erotic fiction, the better written the more effective. Better usually if a little is left to the imagination. I feel it gives me more scope. *Fanny Hill* and D. H. Lawrence are good, particularly in episodes which depict much joy in fucking."

"I get quite a buzz from reading sex-related books—*The Sensuous Couple*, *Sex Without Guilt*, *Surrogate Wife*, *Forum*, etc. I don't read pornographic books. All the ones I have come across were so badly written, I was turned off rather than on," avows our New York airline stewardess.

For Linda, the English girl, "the most erotic passages I have ever read were in *Fanny Hill*, especially where the youth is swimming in the pool and he makes love to the girl who was watching him. The first seduction in *Lady Chatterley* was very exciting, and passages in *Under the Hill*, a very old book, I can't remember who by, especially where Tantalus has a good few sessions with Venus in Paradise. Modern sexy books do little for me, but a set of books by Robert Graham (is it??), *The Sewing-machine Man*, *The Courier*, and *The Debt Collector* were sexy for me as all the four-letter words are used in the same context I am used to hearing them."

Phyllis, the American, reacts to "any artistic and not too blatant description of the sex acts between men and women, or between women, very strongly. Most important is the description of the feelings of the people involved. There are numerous examples—*Lady Chatterley's Lover*, *Couples*—Updike, *The Sot Weed Factor*—John Barth, in particular the description of the rape scene aboard the ship carrying virgins from England to the Colonies. Frances Parkinson Keyes' *Madame Castel's Lodger Crest Book*, paperback edition, pages 143 and 144. From 'By the dim light this gave . . . realms of rapture.' But especially, 'He locked her in his arms and with lips against hers and his heart beating against hers, took her with him into the realms of rapture.' "

"Books definitely turn me on sexually," says May, an English girl. "They can arouse me from nothing. Actual descriptions of stroke-by-stroke action are guaranteed. I have a vivid imagination, and can identify easily. I can't think of any specific examples, but the more extreme, the more effective, e.g., copulation with animals, incest, rape."

"I've read a few sexy books," writes Betty, the American schoolgirl. "I found *Candy* in my brother's room. I've got some books like that of my own. I get very horny reading the sexy parts in a book called *The Exhibitionist*."

Jane, of London, England, enjoys reading books which bring in sexual situations. "I once read a book called *The Song of the Loon*. This was all about homosexuality between North American Indians, and this book, which described fellatio between young Indians, made me incredibly randy."

I have mentioned that a very large number of men are turned on by watching or reading about lesbian sex-acts, and that all the Danish "live shows" begin with such an act, because it was quickly discovered that nothing made the predominantly male audiences more receptive to heterosexual and other acts. There is also some evidence in my material that some women are turned on by watching or reading about male homosexual sex-acts. Though Kinsey has a section on "Observing Portrayals of Sexual Action" in his report on the female—but not on the male—he refers only to human heterosexual activities and animal activities. It is fairly well established that male arousal by watching lesbian acts is not a recent manifestation; but since 68 percent of all females who watch sexual activity are never roused by it according to Kinsey, it would be interesting to know if this interest in male homosexual activity is yet another result of the increase in the woman's recognition of her own sexuality.

Margaret, of Washington, D. C., would have had to answer "No" to the question had she been asked a week or two earlier. "But, not long ago, I read _The Happy Hooker_ by Xaviera Hollander, and I found parts of it so arousing that I could not keep from masturbating while I was reading. These passages are such pure eroticism that I don't see how anyone could fail to be aroused by them. I found myself imagining I was in her place."

I have long been an opponent of romantic novels, because I believe that they lead housewives, who read them as an escape from the drab surroundings of the kitchen and the washing machine and fretful kids, to believe that romantic notions are the mainstay of the human relationship. Not only that they paint a very false picture of reality, but do so in such a fashion that the reader believes in it, and allows it to foster her discontent with her own situation. I am quite convinced that at certain social levels, the reading of romantic novels by wives is the cause of a very great deal of marital friction. I am wondering now, however, in view of what Jeannine of Birmingham, Alabama, says, whether I should not revise my attitudes somewhat.

"Written descriptions of lovemaking in romantic novels rouse me sexually very much. I also find similar situations in some of the short stories in _Cosmopolitan_ magazine which have the same effect. The lovemaking is frequently described from the woman's point of view. Most such stories in other magazines are written from the man's point of view. What rouses me is my being able to imagine myself in the role of the woman. Only stories written from a woman's point of view are able to depict my sexual needs and desires."

Dawn, another American, prefers fact to fiction. "Reading factual accounts or stories of persons' sexual or love lives does turn me on immensely. I am not roused if the stories are of 'sick' persons, but only if they are about persons with 'good' experiences. This is why I read *Forum*."

Finally, Caroline of Gloucester, England, is turned on by "direct and energetic and precise descriptions of the sexual act. Plenty of four-letter words. Lawrence is a bit too lazy. I like Henry Miller's style. There is no pretense about him, not in that way, anyway."

This liking of Caroline's for "direct and energetic and *precise* descriptions" raises a point. We are constantly being told by the Lord Longfords and Mary Whitehouses of this world that the frankness, openness and lack of mystery with which the new "permissive" attitudes are revealing sex are depriving it of much of the excitement which both male and female derived from the "unknown." I recall very vividly a much senior friend of mine, the late Dr. Derry of Durham prison in England—he was in attendance at the very distressing execution of Mrs. Edith Thompson for being an accessory to her husband's murder, and was never the same again—recounting to me once the sexual thrill he got from the sight of a woman's ankle when he was a young man at the beginning of the century, and his comment, "But what was the good of having a stiff prick if one really didn't know what one could do with it, except put it in a woman's cunt. It was more thrilling to fantasize and wank." It is my firm belief, and experience, that "mystery" prevents one from reaching the fullest sexual fulfillment. Only when one knows what the sexual apparatus of both sexes are capable of, only when there is the most open and full discussion of this potential between the partners can theory be put into practice to the greatest advantage of both.

ii. Music

This is clearly what may be termed a "specialized" stimulant. I mean by this that the tone-deaf are obviously not going to be turned on by any music they hear, while I believe that the appreciation of music to the extent that it draws out a sexual response demands a sensitivity a little out of the ordinary. There are definitely some people who have what I term a "sexual wavelength" as far as music goes, but they are a smallish minority. Music which arouses sexually has to be on this wavelength, which, in fact, is a trigger for sexual arousal. Unless the music tunes in exactly, the response is not automatic.

Music is quite different in its triggering effects from what I call eulalation, i.e., sounds which are explicitly sexual, like heavy breathing, moans, whimpers, and shrill cries which have such a heavy sexual content that one knows instinctively that they are made by sexually active people. Evidence shows that there are very few average people who do *not* respond to eulalation. On the other hand, there are people who are roused sexually by a guitar sonata and others who are not, and those who are aroused—for some strange reason—by *The Bluebells of Scotland* and those who are turned off by it.

Taken by and large, women are more nervously sensitive—except possibly in the sexual context—than most men, and because of this are more receptive to musical suggestion than most men are. There ought, then, to be some women who are turned on by music.

Let's see how many, and what they say in justification.

Somewhat surprisingly, a little over half (104) of my 198 collaborators have a sexual response to music of one kind or another. This is not to say that they are all sexually aroused from scratch by this or that piece of music; a number claim that if they make love to certain pieces, their enjoyment of sexual activity and particularly of the climax are greatly intensified. The type of music, of course, depends on their general preferences.

For Margy, the sixteen-year-old English girl, "it has to be rock music. Not that any of the guys I've had would particularly like that in the background. Anyone over twenty-five just doesn't turn on to it. A really good, solid beat with lots of fast electric guitar is fantastic to fuck to. I've only been lucky enough to enjoy the experience once, but it was beautiful. I go to lots of rock concerts and if the band is really good, I end up rushing to the loo to finish myself off. That's what made me go for my 'virgin' guy. He's in a group, which even if it is only amateur, turns out a really good sound."

Bessie, the Texas housewife, twenty-nine, wants it "soft and low. Love is blues." Light blues and jazz with alto sax has a definite rousing effect on another American, eighteen-year-old Chrissie, but she also turns on to Liszt's "Hungarian Rhapsody No. 2," and Rimsky-Korsakov's *Scheherezade*. In fact, "any kind almost, except bubble-gum" draws a response from her.

Clarice, another London, England, schoolgirl has, in contrast, one particular song, "Joy" by Apollo 100, "which turns me inside out," while Audrey from Arlington, Virginia, has more than one: " 'One' by Three Dog Night (from the album *Golden Biscuits*) and 'Tapestry' by Carole King have a fantastic effect on me and my lover when we're alone. Whatever it is, it must be soft and mellow."

Susan, nineteen, American, prefers "romantic music while I'm being laid, it adds to the mood. The music listened to by most people is hard rock. This is no kind of music to be listening to. One of my guys preferred it, and occasionally I used to let him play it, but he always fell into the beat when a down side came on and used to pretend his cock was a drumstick. I used to be really in trouble then."

Wendy, from Mobile, Alabama, by contrast, prefers "fast body-moving music. I can dance for a while and I'm so teased, it's not funny. But then, my kind of dancing is all but laying down and fucking."

For Peggy, of Chicago, it's " 'The Love Death' from Wagner's *Tristan and Isolde*. I try to time my orgasm to occur simultaneously with that climax, and when it happens (sometimes) it's out of this world."

Cassandra of San Diego, California, is only roused by music used as a prelude to lovemaking. "Some music and words are erotic, but during lovemaking it's a damn distraction. I'd rather hear my lover's voice and heartbeat than all the music in the world."

Marilyn, from Richmond, Virginia, also does not like music during lovemaking, but for another reason. "Music can half calm me, and being calm makes me more relaxed and desire lovemaking more. However, once lovemaking starts, I lose my sense of hearing almost completely, and seldom hear anything. My lover must repeat things he says to me, and all outside noises and sounds are obscured."

Edith, from Dundee, Scotland, turns on to quite a large repertoire:

    (a) "Lay, Lady, Lay"—Bob Dylan.
    (b) "Frank Lloyd Wright"—Simon and Garfunkel (*Bridge Over Troubled Waters*).
    (c) Last movement *1812 Overture*.
    (d) "Anglesea—Cat Stevens (*Catch Bull at Four*).
    (e) "The Look of Love"—Burt Bacharach.
    (f) Most music performed by Osibisa.

Joanne, the young English newlywed, is "very excited by all Tom Jones' songs, and the race-part music from *A Man and a Woman*, 'Knights in White Satin' by the Moody Blues, and 'A Whiter Shade of Pale' by Procol Harum."

"Violins and romantic music turn me off," says Linda (English). "But give me primitive music with a strong rhythm that will take over my body when I close my eyes, and a partner who also responds to it, and there are fireworks and bells ringing in no time."

Iris, the Canadian who is deeply in love with the drummer Bill, reacts similarly. "Music is a big thing with me, and it has to be heavy for sex. Santana's music, 'Black Magic Woman,' 'Oye Como Va,' and so on. They use a great deal of drum rhythm and it's beautiful when you lose your senses to the pounding and your whole body moves instinctively with the beat. It's an actual high without drugs or booze. And the climax—God!"

I know what she means, but my turning on music is *Concierto de Aranjuiz for Guitar and Orchestra* by Rodrigo. There's no accounting for tastes!

iii. Discussing Sexual Matters

The response to this is varied, as is to be expected, but more than two-thirds (146 of the 198) do find it stimulating to the point of arousal. For the most part, these discussions take place usually between the partners while in a sexual situation, and are usually restricted to an exchange of requests for caresses that each would like the one to give the other, and talking over past sexual experiences. Eighty-two of the 146 come into this category.

Here is a selection of the more interesting topics discussed by the remaining 64.

"I get very roused if I overhear someone talking about his or her sexual experiences and they do not know I can hear them. It is embarrassing to admit, but I used to be on a party line, and I used to secretly listen in on the telephone conversations of one of my neighbors. She was probably only about nineteen or twenty and she was single. From what I could tell from the very graphic conversations she had with her boyfriends and girlfriends she must have had a very active sex-life. Almost every night she was on the phone talking to one of her girlfriends about boys and about the things she had done with one of her boyfriends, one of her favorite things was to talk about what she was going to do when he came over to visit her. Hearing her talking about these things always got me very roused. I like to talk about sexual matters with other people, but it does not rouse me as much as overhearing people talking about sex." (American.)

This is a kind of aural voyeurism which is common to a fair number of women. It takes a number of forms, like the following, for example.

"Some of my girlfriends and I talk about sex a whole bunch. We talk about boys and what we've done with them. We talk about what our boyfriends are like when we play around with them. We talk about how big our boyfriends' cocks are when they're hard. Who has the biggest, who has the smallest. (It's a real put down to have a boyfriend with a cock like a little boy's.) It turns me on to hear what other girls do with boys, and to tell them what I do." (American schoolgirl.)

Or, "Talking with another woman about a man whom we both think is sexy generally rouses me sexually. If the other woman I am talking with knows him better than I do about what kind of lover he is, it rouses me sexually to hear what she knows about him, as long as what she knows is good." (American.)

Or, "Sometimes I will get into a discussion with one of my married friends about sex, and I get aroused by hearing about her sex-life with her husband." (American.)

Or, "About how he would like to lick me till I go crazy and beg for it. When he tells me about some of the things he's done with other women." (American.)

Others, like this English schoolgirl, get sexual kicks out of describing their own activities, getting their kicks from the ignorance of their audience that they are talking about themselves. She has lesbian tendencies, also is bisexual.

"There is a game I play with my 'girlfriend.' It turns us both on and at the same time gives us a laugh. You see, in our 5th form at a girl' grammar school [the class second from top in a state high school] only 4 out of 32 have fucked or done any-

131

thing sexual at all. Therefore, the others tend to look on us as very knowledgeable. That in itself is funny because, my God, don't I know that I've got a hell of a lot left to discover.

"Well, anyway, they like to bring up the subject of sex just to see what my friend and I have to say about it. Our favourite turn-on is to bring up lesbianism and bisexuality. Don't those girls wince at the thought! It's very funny to hear them. 'Oh! Isn't it disgusting!' 'How could they?' 'But what can they do to each other?'

"My friend pretends that she dislikes the idea, whereas I start saying how nice it sounds. She then mentions that her aunt is as bent as can be. 'But I'd never have guessed,' she says. 'She's never made a pass at me.' That's my cue to say, 'Christ! Who in their right minds would want you?' At this point we have a difficult job keeping straight faces.

"We continue discussing the subject, but everything we say relates to us. We sit there giving each other 'looks,' both getting really turned on. The best thing is that none of the others realise we are talking about ourselves. If they knew, it would spoil it, and we wouldn't get turned on."

Some, like another English schoolgirl, use it as a kind of cock-teasing.

"In class my boyfriend and I tell one another what we're going to do to each other after school, like I'll say, 'Richard (which is what we call his cock) is going to get a surprise,' and I tell him what I'm going to do, and it goes on like that."

Or, "It all depends what you mean, I'll talk

about sex, whatever particular thing I choose, in an erotic way if I want to turn a guy on and as a result get turned on myself." (English schoolgirl.)

This is a kind of seduction technique, when used as this English girl uses it.

"To a certain extent I get turned on by discussing sexual matters, but especially if I know what I am saying is exciting the man I'm talking to. Relating my sexual adventures or listening to someone else's (male or female) is very exciting, but unfortunately it mostly happens in pubs or at work, and so can only occasionally be followed by sexual activity. Seduction (rather than mutual consent) by one person is even better. A female friend of mine related how she planned and achieved the seduction of a man ten years her junior. All the time I had to appear interested but cool, but I would have been much more excited if I could have asked her questions."

Or, "I get quite a buzz discussing sexual matters with men. When men realise I am married, they frequently make some effort to find out whether I sleep with other men as well. The conversations always have a very subtle initiation. 'What does your husband think about your flying around on airplanes, and being gone so much of the time?' It generally leads round to, 'Wonder what he does with you gone away so much?' followed by, 'What would you do if you discovered he was sleeping with someone else while you're away?' From my answer they hope to learn whether or not I sleep around myself. Sometimes I give an honest reply, sometimes not. I would *very infrequently* get into such a conversation with a passenger, but with a pilot it is not so rare."

"I have several friends I can share my fantasies with and they with me. All but one or two are men. I am very aroused by hearing these fantasies and knowing the masturbation practices of my friends. These friends also are people I like to share sexual dreams with."

Some use it deliberately as an arousal technique, or a kind of fantasy to which to masturbate, when the lovers are separated by distances.

"Almost any kind of sexual talk arouses me—especially when my love threatens me playfully. Or, on the phone, when he tells me that our sexy conversation has given him an erection, and then goes into great detail about what he would do to me if I were there. I can tell by his voice—he gets a bit breathless—when he's balling himself, and that really turns me on, so I bring myself off, too. We both know we do this, but we've never mentioned it yet." (American.)

Let Jan, the veteran of 70 affairs, again have the last word.

"This can be considered in two contexts. One would be discussing sexual matters in a sexual context (i.e., naked and in bed after sex, and waiting for further sexual activity) and the other would be in a nonsexual context (i.e., dressed and having a discussion pure and simple).

"I find the former much more rousing than the

latter. The latter may be interesting or informative, but it is too objective and explicit to rouse me. I don't mind the latter type at all, but it is too objective and explicit to rouse me.

"The former, however, can be rousing. After sex, I find guys often want to discuss sexual matters, e.g., how would I rate them as lovers, were they as good or better than most, am I glad we met, etc., etc.? This I frequently find rousing. It also gives me a feeling of power, but I am always careful not to knock a guy in this situation."

iv. Fantasies or Erotic Thoughts

Superior sexual beings that they consider themselves to be, men have for long believed that most women are no match for them in sexual imagination. Nancy Friday has definitely exploded this myth with her book, *My Secret Garden: Women's Sexual Fantasies*, and my collaborators have provided me with magnificent material to support her thesis.

Again, it would be interesting to know if this development of the sexual imagination—which I believe to be one of the most important sexual attributes a woman or man can have—is part of the recent process of the discovery by women of their own sexuality, or has always existed. There is a vast body of evidence, going back for many centuries, that men have fantasized, not only when they masturbate, but frequently when they fuck; there is no similar evidence from the pens of women.

Kinsey considers fantasizing under three headings—which strikes me as being rather narrow: (i) fantasies concerning opposite sex, (ii) fantasies concerning own sex, and (iii) fantasies during masturbation. The conclusions he reached were that whereas 84 percent of all males admitted to being aroused by fantasies involving women, only 69 percent of females had ever had erotic fantasies about males, 31 percent insisting that they never fantasized erotically at all. Those women who did fantasize did so infrequently, while the men fantasized more frequently. Homosexual males fantasize about other males in the same numbers as those heterosexuals who fantasize about women, but lesbians are far less numerous, only 28 percent fantasizing with erotic response frequently, 46 percent with some response and 26 percent never fantasized with erotic response.

But it is in the fantasies accompanying masturbation in which the difference is more definitely and clearly seen. Seventy-two percent of the total of 93 percent of masturbating males always fantasize when they masturbate, but only 50 percent of 62 percent of masturbating females fantasize every time they masturbate. Put in another way, roughly 69 out of every 100 males always have erotic fantasies while masturbating, but only 31 out of every 100 females always have erotic fantasies while masturbating. Since fantasizing while masturbating is the most frequent use of erotic fantasizing, these last figures give a fair idea of the fantasizing incidence of men and women.

Only 9 of my 198 never fantasize or deliberately use erotic thoughts as stimuli. This works out at roughly 4 out of every 100 women, as against Kinsey's 69 out of every 100 women.

Quite a number of the fantasies concern the sexual partner of the moment, a number concern rape, quite a few involve "bondage" either of the woman or her partner, not often involving sadistic or masochistic acts; and to refute the argument that women have poor sexual imaginations, a number concern really "exotic" situations, which are worked out in great detail. If you want to study this subject in greater depth, read Nancy Friday's book. Here I will content myself with giving a selection of the more imaginative fantasies sent to me by women.

* * * *

"I fantasise about having sex in a sensual or opulent or even decadent setting. In my favourite fantasy, I am a harem girl, and I am brought to the private apartment of the Sultan, who fits exactly my image of a sexy male. We spend the whole night having sex in his huge opulent bed. Lately I have been having a similar fantasy that is just as good; in the fantasy I am the ruler, the Sultana, and I have a harem of men. The men are always real men whom I know or have seen. This fantasy has much more variety than the first one, because I can

137

imagine having sex with one man after another. Each one satisfies my desires in a different way. Occasionally I imagine I have harem girls, too, and that these girls have sex with me, too. More often I imagine that I am secretly watching as one of the girls has sex with one of the men."

* * * *

"Erotic thoughts and fantasies—many. I think of many men masturbating and fucking me at the same time, kissing mouth, breast, clitoris, vagina, anus, and lots of sucking and fucking. I also imagine sex between me and one other female (no one I know) especially cunnilingus with me passive. And cunnilingus with one man who wants only to perform that with me and desires nothing else. Queen fantasies, with many subjects all of whom love me and demonstrate their love by kissing, fucking and sucking."

* * * *

"I often fantasise about throwing a party for all the men I've ever been sexually attracted to. I would look like a million dollars, sexy dress, etc., and they would, of course, be starkers. I'd spend all night rousing them to bursting point one by one, and finish up by using two, to spend the rest of the night in bed with me."

* * * *

"I only fantasise while I masturbate. I have a number of fantasies. In one, another woman is licking and sucking my vagina. In another, people are watching me while I am fucking, in another a film director is making a close-up of me masturbating as I come, and lastly, I am being fucked by many men, and not able to hold back my pleasure."

* * * *

"I suppose I need more experience as I'm only sixteen, but mine are very exotic. They sound quite ordinary, but the effect they have is beautiful.

"I find that mine are about women most of the time. Thinking about guys is a bit more difficult.

"When I was thirteen, I used to have fantasies with just me and one other person, usually a boy. It was private, but now I seem to be adding people from nowhere.

"My closest friend is a girl of my own age. She's really sexy. You know, one of the girls that mothers hate and fathers encourage you to bring home more often. She's got beautiful long blonde hair, really firm, large (39") boobs, very dark pubes, and oozes sex appeal. She figures in a lot of my fantasies.

"In one particular fantasy which I have quite often, if I feel like turning myself on without much effort, I am in a threesome—me, her, and the married man she currently belongs to, and he's fantastic as well. In this fantasy we are in a beautiful flat, very luxurious. The floors are covered with real animal fur, there's no furniture, just lots of sik cushions. We all shower together, but I don't want any contact with her, just him.

"For a while, I do nothing. I just watch as he makes love to her, getting very turned on by just viewing. Then she has an orgasm, but only a very mild one, and he suggests I might have better luck. This is where I get some enjoyment.

"She reluctantly agrees, and then I get to work. I take the active role, whereas she is passive, very passive. I begin with her head and work down to her cunt. She doesn't do anything much, and only begins to show response when I really concentrate on her cunt. I don't imagine it all in minute detail. I just have a hazy picture. When she comes, it's really spectacular—screams, the lot. What I like is the bit when I nastily pinch her nipples. Then I fuck with her guy while she relaxes. Pretty basic, isn't it?

"Sometimes I have incestuous fantasies, but for some stupid reason always feel more than guilty afterwards especially if they helped me have really good orgasms.

"The dream I've just recently started to use concerns my present boyfriend. He's only seventeen, and until I got hold of him, he was still a virgin. What a waste! He's really beautiful; he looks almost like a girl. Anyhow, I imagine him at a party. I'm there, too, but he just ignores me. He finds some sexy bird and they go off to a bedroom. (See, still very ordinary.) I miss out on all the details, but very clearly I can see him coming and her coming at the same time. It's really agonising for me, because when he and I fuck, I just never come. Then I sort of get into his mind. I can hear what he's thinking and it's pretty nasty. He's comparing me with her, and I get a very low rating. It's a really nasty thing, and I'd hate it to happen in real life, but it does turn me on to think about it."

* * * *

"My answer to this question could take up many pages. Mainly, I have two themes. The best is this.

"I am stranded on a desert island, or in a jungle, with a man, black or white, though usually white. He has either been stranded before me, or arrives after me. After two weeks or so of remaining aloof, I agree to share camp with him to help pool resources, or guard against animals or weather or something. I refuse all approaches, pretending I'm naive and don't understand.

"I realise all along I am tormenting him. I deliberately bathe in front of him, sunbathe naked and pretend to need massaging due to a mishap. I refuse to discuss my past so that he will not learn how sexy I am.

"After a couple of months, he begins to show signs of strain and to shake when he comes near me. His attentions become annoying. Then he realises I am not menstruating. I tell him that is because I am on the pill and had six months' supply with me. I am, therefore, taking them continuously as I haven't any Tampax, which would prove difficult on the island.

"At this he becomes very passionate, telling me he had only controlled himself for fear I became pregnant. I laugh at him, still ignoring his obvious need. I continue this for another week. In the end, he breaks down and cries, and begs me to allow him any form of sexual relief, even if just to masturbate while looking at my naked body.

"I act shocked and disgusted, while all along I feel his pain inside me and revel in it. Eventually, just before we are rescued, I allow him to caress my breasts but won't let him kiss me, or have firm sexual contact. We are rescued and he's a physical and mental wreck, and I return to my man, virtue intact and very frustrated for a furiously passionate time in bed.

"As a variation on this theme, sometimes a native appears on the scene, towards the end of the fantasy and I allow him to make love to me, knowing my compatriot's condition is being made worse as he watches us.

"If I am marooned with a black man (a fantasy that is usually brought on by seeing a fantastic coloured chap during the day) then I acquiesce straight away, and can't get enough.

"The other fantasy also involves a coloured fellow and girl, with two or three or four of us in bed. (Never more than four.) We are mutually caressing and making love. I am watching my man making love, and am kissing his penis and licking round it as he enters his girl. All the time I am being gently fucked from behind by a handsome, strong man.

"I do have other fantasies, involving being tied down and having a succession of young men fuck me, until I can't take any more, or I am tempting a young boy to endurance promising everything and denying everything. This excites me very much, the idea of ruining a young boy's chances for life, by laughing at his attempts to satisfy me."

I am not going to analyze the psychological motivations underlying these fantasies. In fact, I am sure there is no need to spell them out for the last one. The woman is twenty-six only.

* * * *

"I have erotic thoughts and fantasies all the time. I would love to be fucked by a black man. My favourite fantasy is I'm on my hands and knees while the big Black with the biggest cock ever is fucking me from behind and I have another Black also with a big hard cock that I am sucking off. He never comes in my mouth, because I like to watch it shoot in the air, then I lick him clean.

"Then I like to straddle a big cock and ride up and down, while he has another broad sitting on his face and he's eating pussy. Or I'm lying on my back while this stud is fucking me and another is straddling me and sucking me."

* * * *

"I fantasise being spanked over my man's knees as correction for being bitchy. I often masturbate to this fantasy or to one in which I'm tied helpless, limbs spreadeagled, to the bed while my man takes his pleasure as he wishes before releasing me and our mutually screwing afterwards. Occasionally I fantasise that I have *him* tied helpless while I tantalise him, putting off his orgasm until *I* decide it is time. In this latter fantasy, I have no desire to inflict pain on him, but to caress and lick at his body until he can't stand it."

* * * *

"Erotic thoughts of my boyfriend and I together or him with another man (he is bisexual) combined with written or photographic porno really get me going and this usually ends up with a session in bed or mutual masturbation."

* * * *

"I have an absentee boyfriend in America who holds my heart, so don't have an awful lot of intercourse when he's not here, and thus have a big need for fantasies. I dominate and seduce and drive men and non-men abstract entities I've never met, or people in power I could never attain. I'm seduced by nonexistent milkmen and generally raped by the lowest of the low. The concept of incest (though I can't imagine it with my real father and have no brothers) appeals to me no end. Most of my fantasies are—obviously—aggressive, by me or against me, and extreme. I'm genuinely not an aggressive person in actuality."

* * * *

I receive numerous letters from women—and men —who are worried because if they fantasize they think they must be kinky. I do not regard fantasizing either as kinky or off-beat, and I tell everyone that if fantasies intensify the sexual experience, they are completely justified. If fantasies replace or exclude the sexual experience then the whole is out of balance. Particularly do I believe that fantasies should always accompany masturbation because they do give meaning to an act that otherwise is coldly physical.

3

Groping Around

••>—⊕>◦<⊕—<••

The body of every man and woman is well supplied with sensitive zones which, if properly caressed, cannot fail to bring the average man and woman to full sexual arousal. The woman's chief sensitive zones are, in order of greatest sensitivity, the clitoris, the sex-lips, and the vagina-entrance. Next comes the nipples, but though the majority of women respond readily to stimulation of them by finger and thumb and the mouth (sucking or licking), there are far more women than is realized who find such attentions to the nipples off-putting by being irritating and sometimes downright painful. Strangely, many of these women are highly stimulated if their partner takes the whole breast in his hand and squeezes until it is slightly painful.

The other sensitive zones are the insides and, to a less extent, the outsides of the upper thighs, the perineum—the ridge between the vagina and the anus—

behind the knees, the lips and the inside of the mouth, the throat, the nape of the neck, behind the ears, the lobes, the length of the spine, the buttocks (for some, the anus), and the navel. There are not many parts of the surface of the body, then, that are not sexually responsive to caresses of one kind or another, principally with the fingers, lips, and tongue. This being so, unlike the responses to psychological stimuli, responses to physiological stimuli, at least via some of the sensitive zones, makes physiological response universal.

This is not the place for me to go into the techniques of physiological stimulation—may I refer you to *The Sensuous Couple* if you want to brush up on these—nor into the possible individual differences in response to stimulation of this or that sensitive zone, but there are certain aspects of the woman's response to physiological stimuli which I thought it would be useful to know.

Once again, except for the physiological caresses of the partner which have a direct physical effect, the other two areas of arousal, while being directly physiological, have psychological overtones. This is particularly true of the woman's caresses of the partner, which although physiological for him, have psychologically arousing properties for her.

There were those areas in which I was particularly interested, because (a) they are to be found in men as well as women and (b) because they will be an indicator of the development of female sexuality, if women more freely and more frequently admit to them nowadays than previously, since they entail a loss of inhibition. The three are (i) the touch or feel of certain objects, (ii) a particular caress by the partner, and (iii) caressing the partner, especially his penis, which produces its physiological responses via the brain.

i. The Touch or Feel of Certain Objects

In my view, to become sexually aroused by the touch or feel of an object which has no direct sexual quality indicates a higher degree of sexual sensitivity and, perhaps, a more ready sexual response than if the response is obtained only, or chiefly, by the partner's stimulation of the sensitive zones.

Let's see how many of our women respond in this way, and what objects stimulate them. Not quite two-thirds (113) of the 198 admit they can be sexually roused in this way. Unfortunately, Kinsey did not explore this area of sexual stimuli so I have no yardstick, but that 113 women out of 198 are sexually aroused by touching or feeling primarily nonsexual objects does seem to me to express a higher sexual sensitivity among women than we have hitherto acknowledged.

Let's see what some of the objects are.

Since the contact of skin against skin is highly sensual and sexually arousing, it is not surprising that many women are sexually stimulated by the touch of soft materials, such as velvet, silk, and fur, brushed against the naked skin. Several of the women who react to silk or nylon have silk sheets for their beds, or intend to get them when they marry. Women who respond to the touch of fur have no inhibitions preventing them from making love on a fur rug either on the bed or the floor with an abandon far in excess of their usual response to lovemaking. Flowing water, especially over the genitals, is another surefire stimulant for many, and so is swimming completely naked.

As I have said, however, it is not surprising that materials akin to human skin in their smoothness and softness should draw sexual response from many women—as they do for many men—but there are among the objects declared to me, some that are surprising.

* * * *

"Touch? YES. Hot, cold, rough, smooth, etc., etc. I would be more than grateful if you could reply to this and send me some information on *synthesis*. I do definitely feel/see colours. Different areas of my body with different colours according to heavy/light touches, different materials and textures and shapes, and mainly according to my level of arousal. It happens only rarely, but I've taken comprehensive notes of it for several years and when it does happen it follows a similar pattern."

* * * *

"I'd like to roll in fur stark naked. Also scratchier stuff, like hessian, would definitely turn me on."

* * * *

"The feel of dead skins, etc., and velvet sends shivers up my spine, and makes me feel in need of a man to kiss and touch me. It doesn't make me feel randy."

* * * *

"I like to have cold cream spread thickly across my stomach, and then see people's fingers digging into it. That can bring me off on its own."

* * * *

"Sealskin, a peach in my hand, fine knitted nylon, certain washing-up cloths, *real* sponge, and chamois leather, I find all very rousing."

* * * *

"Only the touch of coarse hands. That makes me randy in no time."

* * * *

"Velvet and fur I find sexually stimulating and now, to quite a great extent, leather and rubber, largely because these latter materials have become associated with a particular man with whom I have what I consider to be the perfect love relationship and who finds them sexually exciting. I have found him quite wonderful in bed when wearing these materials."

* * * *

"To touch velvet being worn by a man I find appealing and very rousing. Otherwise, velvet doesn't do a thing for me."

*　*　*　*

"Taking a warm, fragrant bubble bath frequently arouses me sexually. Another thing is the feel of the wind. Sometimes when it is windy, I take off all my clothes and go out into the garden, and I always have to finish up masturbating. It's even better if there is a light rain."

*　*　*　*

"I am sexually aroused by touching (and eating) bananas and mushrooms."

(The significance of bananas I can see, but not of mushrooms. Am I being very dense?)

*　*　*　*

I have excluded the touch of skin, because it is perhaps the most physiological stimulant to both the toucher and the touched. However, I thought I would include the following, because the lady may have several points.

"What I like best is to feel a man's bare bottom. Also, after I have started to become aroused, I like to cup his balls in my hand and feel their weight, which really brings me on. The soft and smooth, but firm, head of his penis after it's erect has the same effect, and even more so if I feel it with my tongue and lips."

ii. One Particular Caress by the Partner?

I really included this question to indicate to men that they may not know exactly which caress turns their partner on, unless the partner is frank enough (or uninhibited enough) to tell them. I also wondered whether we men might learn about caresses that would never occur to us in a month of Sundays.

Every woman of the 198 had at least one caress that never failed to arouse her and bring her off. For 49 (or nearly 1 in 4) this was manual stimulation of the clitoris, and for 40 (or about 1 in 5) it was cunnilingus. Of the remaining 109, 41 mentioned the effectiveness of cunnilingus,* but each had, too, one special caress which made them randy, and which, in some cases, could bring them off without direct stimulation of the genitals.

I propose, now, to give some of the more esoteric caresses which the 109 have recorded.

* * * *

"Pushing his prick up my anus."

* * * *

---

* This figure, added to the 40 for whom cunnilingus is *the* caress, means that nearly *half* of the sample are known to find oral sex acceptable. Even if the remaining half do not—but I should be surprised if a good number did not accept oral sex—I suggest that this is an indication that tremendous inroads have been made into women's opposition to oral sex, opposition which was based for the most part on feelings of shame, and that it was kinky, and a belief that it was dirty.

"(a) Running a finger or tongue along my waist line, down to my hipbones, back to waist, back to hip bones, etc., etc., until I say 'get on with it,' or words to that effect.

"(b) Any caress he cares to give my body."

* * * *

"I have three particular ones:

"(a) I love having my ears eaten. The best part is when the tongue penetrates into the ear.

"(b) I like to have the part of my neck just about the right shoulder bone bitten and licked.

"(c) *I practically come if my fingers are lightly bitten from the tips to the base and then having my arms bitten up to the elbow.*" [Italics mine—R.C.]

* * * *

"Depends who I'm with actually. The guy I want to marry is a fingers man. The guy I almost married was a lips man. I could kiss or merely be kissed by him for ever. My husband-to-be can be *so* unbelievably gentle with his hands, and so unbelievably *patient*.

"The first night we went out, he took three-quarters of an hour to work round from behind my armpit, to my nipple along the line of my bra, micromillimeter by micromillimeter, yet always moving sufficiently to keep me aroused and not let me get adapted and *so, so* gentle.

"He does the same to me all over the lips of my vagina and inside and out and on and on forever, and I rise so very slowly and yet realising that I can

154

go on rising until eternity, and anticipating, and finally he will plunge in a finger, two fingers hard and go on from there, and/or a special thrill, a sudden twist of the hand so that the wristbone grates suddenly, harshly against the soft sensitive insides of the tops of my thighs."

* * * *

"I love him to run his hands over and under my ass while we're screwing at the same time that we're kissing."

* * * *

"The running of his tongue round the inside of my teeth makes me as randy as anything else he can do."

* * * *

"One particular caress—standing—when you are held so close and tight you can feel all the male is blessed with—cock and balls—fitting so comfortably between your legs."

* * * *

"I love to have my tits played with. I get really turned on when a boy sucks on them. I've only had it done to me twice [she's only sixteen] by the same boy, but I got turned on more than any other time in my life when he got down and did it with his mouth. I came both times without him doing anything else. When a boy does it to me down there with his fingers, it feels real good, but I don't come."

* * * *

"When he's fondling my breasts while kissing them, and at the same time making me come manually. (It sounds so cold and clinical when typed, but in real life we're anything but.)"

* * * *

"Gentle biting at the back of the neck to either side brings me off on its own."

* * * *

"My lover caresses every inch of my body, but when he brushes my vagina with his penis, it is the most glorious moment of all his caresses. He knows how much I enjoy this moment and prolongs entrance as long as I can stand it."

* * * *

"There is no particular caress, unless initial entry can be termed a 'caress.' I think it can, because the touch of his penis at my entrance makes me leap forward towards coming with a big jump."

* * * *

"He has taught me to love one thing that he does. He makes me stand perfectly still, and then kisses me in the mouth, ordering me not to respond until I must. It's sheer agony, and then all orders and rules go by the board. He has a lover's imagination that I have never known in anyone else . . .

until I read about some of the things in *Forum*."

* * * *

"Having my breasts and nipples caressed arouses me very much and can soon bring me off. I especially like to have a man take one of my nipples into his mouth. I could and have spent much time having a man do that to me. Second to that is cunnilingus which arouses me about as much."

* * * *

"After making love I especially like to lie on my partner facing him and have him caress my back and buttocks. I also like touching my partner's face while making love and have him touch mine."

* * * *

"Having the area of my clitoris and vagina caressed makes me respond more than anything else. One way of doing that, which is difficult for a man to do, but which I get most pleasure from, is having that area caressed with the top of his penis. If he cannot do that, doing it with his tongue is just about as good."

* * * *

" 'Sixty-nine' brings us both on more than anything else. Standing in the shower with the water and soap falling off us is great and also good clean fun."

* * * *

"Occasionally, if I lift my skirt when we are together in the car, he will, in spite of himself (not wishing to be roused when he can't complete the act) reach over and caress my cunt and later put his fingers in his mouth. (Two other men have done this same thing in the past under the same circumstances.) It's almost as though it were an unconscious reflex action. It excites me almost to the point of coming when he puts his finger in his mouth. Could it be because it indicates an acceptance of my sexuality as no other gesture could do in restricted circumstances?"

* * * *

Each one of us, if we ever tried to find out what it was, would discover, I think, that we have some special preference outside the more usual caresses. It is worthwhile, I believe, spending some time in searching, always remembering that a caress you may bestow on yourself takes on an entirely different and more intense quality when bestowed by a partner. If, therefore, you discover on your own that a certain caress in a certain spot is exciting, you may be sure that the same caress from a partner will excite you even more. In sex, never take anything for granted.

* * * *

Krystyna is thirty-four, a Swede married to an Englishman, and lives in Sussex, England.

"We have a heated swimming pool, where we can swim naked all the year round. We often make love while we are swimming. It's quite surprising the number of different things you can do. When there is just Max and I, there are two positions that we use, each of which I find especially exciting and which give me fantastic orgasms. In one I lie on my tummy holding on to the steps, which are at the shallow end. When he kneels down in the water Max's penis is exactly level with my vagina. So he kneels between my legs and comes into me, and then puts his hand round and parts my sex-lips. He doesn't touch my clitoris at all. Then we rock backwards and forwards, and the movement of the water over my clitoris is indescribable. It takes a long time for me to come off like this, because the build-up is slow. It may take more than a quarter of an hour, but all the time there are these superb sensations which slowly get more and more intense, until there is a huge burst, which makes me tremble like a leaf from fingertips to toes. Max always holds out until I begin to tremble, then he brings himself off and the jerking of his penis inside me, makes me tremble even more, and the more I tremble, the more intense my sensations are. I have blacked out coming off like this, which I have never done when we make love in bed or anywhere else.

"Another way we do it is to go into deeper water, so that Max's feet are firmly touching the bottom and his shoulders are above the water. Then I climb on to his penis and put my legs round his waist, and cross my feet. I think if you do it on land like this, they call it The Tree. When Max bends his knees and straightens them, his penis goes in and out of my vagina and as it does so, it makes the water flow under a kind of pressure between my sex-lips and over my clitoris, and this is fantastic, too.

"But most fantastic of all is when we do it at the water inlet. This is in the shallow end, and the water flows in very, very strongly. I face the inlet and hang on to the sides, then with my knees apart I squat down until my sex-lips are exactly opposite the end about six or seven inches away. Max kneels behind me and comes in. The underwater jet forces my sex-lips open and plays directly on my clitoris. It also hits the base of Max's penis which doesn't come in me, and joggles his balls about, which he finds very exciting. We both come off very quickly, but I always have seven or eight orgasms, and Max never fewer than two. His second one always takes longer than the first, which is why I have so many more orgasms than Max. But once when Max was particularly randy he had three in about three minutes, and then had two more slower ones. I lost count of mine that time. We had to go and lie on the bed afterwards, we were completely exhausted. But it was a fantastic experience.

"Sometimes Allan and Richard come and swim with us, and they like helping us and watching us. Allan and Richard are bisexual, like Max. Sometimes I let them make love to me if they haven't brought their girlfriends with them, which quite often they don't. Sometimes Allan and Richard make love together, and this I find terribly exciting. So does Max. We often sit on the side and watch them.

Just seeing an erect penis under the water and being moved about by it, turns me on tremendously.

"The way Allan and Richard like best for making love, is for them to face one another and put their penises between each other's thighs and thrusting. They say that their penises rub against one another as well as against their thighs, and that's what really excites them. While they are doing this, they deep kiss one another really passionately. This turns me on, too. Sometimes they sit on the edge of the pool deep-kissing and stroking one another's penises, and I have sometimes come off just watching them. When they come off in the pool, you can see their semen shooting through the water like little puffs of smoke. If Max just touches my nipples when we are watching this, I come off at once.

"We once gave a group party in the pool, but it wasn't a great success. It was too noisy, and with a lot of people threshing about it churned up the water so much, it got in people's mouths and made them choke.

"Recently Max and I have decided we mustn't make love in the pool as often as we have been doing. We've begun to find that we are not having such intense orgasms when we make love in the house as we used to, and we think it's because it is always so exciting in the pool that we are coming to rely on it too much. I hope you don't think we're too kinky, Dr Chartham, but you always say there should be no holds barred in sex."

Krystyna has understood me absolutely correctly. I do say that it does not matter how people behave sexually with one another, but I do insist that *all* concerned shall find the behavior acceptable, both physically and psychologically. So, in this sense, there are some holds barred. But I would not bar any that Krystyna has described.

iii. Caressing the Partner

As I have explained, being sexually roused by caressing a partner while drawing his responses from him via his body, makes you respond, if you do respond, via your brain. In other words, his responses are physiological while yours are psychological.

The point of my question, however, was to find out if women are, in general, stimulated by their caressing the partner; for if they were, it would be one more argument in support of my contention that women are as responsive psychologically as men so obviously are.

I asked if touching the penis had any special arousal qualities, because it seemed to me that an erection, being an indisputable sign that the man is already aroused, might have strong psychological arousal qualities for the woman. If touching a man's penis excited a woman more than touching him anywhere else, it would strengthen the viewpoint that women must play at least an equal role in physical lovemaking, because she helps to arouse herself thereby, and so assists her partner. In the past, many women have shown reluctance to fondle or stimulate, touch, or even look at the partner's penis during lovemaking. Where this has occurred—and my files on the complaints of late middle-aged husbands against their wives contain a large number of letters on this point—in most cases the woman has invariably had difficulty in reaching orgasm, often never reaching it at all. Psychological factors obviously played a role in some cases in this refusal to touch the penis—unconscious fear of sex, active dislike of sex, conscious or unconscious fear of pregnancy, and so on—but in many cases it was ignorance of the effect of the physiological stimulus on the man and of the psychological stimulus on herself that made the woman hold back from caressing the penis. This was, at the same time, a reflection on her own understanding and acceptance of her own sexuality. On the other hand, if our 198 women not only caressed the penis but were stimulated themselves by doing so, it would be another indication of the development of female sexuality.

About a quarter (54) made no reference to the penis, and indicated that though they were aroused by caressing the partner, they were not so aroused as by his caresses of them. Of the remaining 144, arousal by touching the penis was surefire, though some had a preference for other caresses. Fellatio, when practiced, was always highly exciting, and even more women were aroused—some to the point of orgasm, as with fellatio—by feeling the penis become erect in their hands. (I won't give a breakdown of these figures, because statistics can become very tedious.) However, "groping a guy" generally turns a significant number on, many getting more excited by doing it through clothes than in the nude.

"I get very horny," says Carol of Wilmington, North Carolina, "when I feel my guy's balls through his trousers and his cock getting a hard-on while I'm doing it. I do it sometimes when we're out driving, and when his cock is stiff, I unzip his fly and take it out and go down on him, while he's still driving. I always come off when I'm doing this, sometimes before he does."

On the whole, though, women find caressing the naked male most arousing.

"I enjoy moving my tongue slowly all over his body, gradually getting nearer and nearer his cock. When I get quite near, his cock begins to jump and when I actually touch the tip of it lightly with my tongue-tip it leaps up and hits me in the mouth. If he touched my clit then, I'd come immediately."

There are some accounts of response reactions to more out-of-the-ordinary caresses which might be helpful in experimenting with the partner to discover his particular likes and dislikes.

* * * *

"I am very aroused by rubbing his penis against my face. It is also extremely exciting to rub the tip against my nipple until he comes. The spurting of his semen on my nipple, never fails to bring me off."

* * * *

"If a guy has nice juicy nipples, I turn on at once when I see them. But fellating him is best. When I did it to my virgin the first time, he thought he was in another planet. That really helped my ego, which, in turn, inspired my cunt."

* * * *

"I only like caressing my partner when he doesn't just want to get his nuts off, but makes me feel wanted."

* * * *

"I get very turned on when he dangles his semi-erect penis over my nipples, and gets hard by my rubbing it against them. When he rubs my nipples with his penis it isn't the same, not so electric."

* * * *

"There's something very satisfying about going to sleep with a cuntful of prick. Even when I've already come off, sometimes I come off a second time as he lies behind me and I reach between my legs and rub the head of his prick between my sex-lips and then suddenly push it in."

* * * *

"I get super randy when I bring him off with my hands, more so than when I suck him."

* * * *

"My partner is so anal erotic that I've overcome

my earlier inhibitions and now find analinctus to be powerfully stimulating to me."

* * * *

"If I caress him from the tip of his cock with my tongue, and go down over his balls to his anus and back, it gives me almost as much physical excitement as it does him."

((The perineum is a much neglected sensitive zone. More should be caressing it.)

* * * *

"What rouses me most is seeing that my caresses are rousing him."

* * * *

"When I flick my tongue rapidly on the underside of Guy's penis just below the tip, it makes his penis jump so that it seems alive. Seeing, or rather feeling this 'live' thing moving like this turns me on more than his responses to anything else that I can do to him, and he's only got to touch my clitoris once while I'm doing it and his penis is jumping to bring me off immediately."

* * * *

"Ron goes mad if I make him lie on his back, and I kneel over him facing his feet. I put him in me, then I make him draw up both knees, and I pick up one foot and bring it across to the other knee, and I suck his big toe. This makes him shout and wriggle and in about a couple of minutes he comes off. Almost before he's finished coming, he's pushed me off and mounted me, and thrusts until he comes again, which doesn't take him very long. He does this all very roughly. He seems to go right out of his mind. But afterwards he's very gentle and sweet, and asks me to forgive him. I haven't told him yet that I like doing this to him because it gives me a sense of power over him to make him so roused that he more or less loses control, and that when he 'attacks' me, he brings me off much more intensely than when he makes love to me gently, and his being sorry afterwards just makes me feel all the more superior. But this feeling of power and superiority frightens me a little, so I don't do it to him very often. I usually save it for when he's been a little bit beastly to me, and I want to get my own back. Would you call me a sadist, Dr. Chartham?"

There are one or two traits of sadism in what you do, but I don't think you need worry about them. After all, you are giving Guy, to judge by his responses, a really intense sexual experience, which he clearly enjoys; and at the same time, fortunately, you are having a special experience yourself, which does even things out a little, I think. I should begin to worry about you if you ever did tell him what your motives were and then carried on doing it, because then you would destroy him sexually. In my view there is no greater sexual crime than one partner deliberately destroying the other sexually. As things are, you have done neither

Guy nor yourself any harm. On the contrary, you are doing both of you a lot of good, so keep it that way.

* * * *

"Do you know any man whose most sensitive zone is his buttocks, more sensitive even than his cock? I do. I can play for hours with Tristan's cock, and go down on him for eternity and he won't get a hard-on, but if I gently stroke his buttocks his cock comes up in seconds. Do you know, that if he comes into me and I stroke his buttocks, he comes off in no time at all without moving.

"I didn't know about this when we first met, and I got him to go to bed with me. He was a shy guy and seemed very reluctant to lay me. But I got him there eventually, and then nothing happened, because his cock just would not get hard whatever I did. He was nearly out of his mind and weeping, and I felt so sorry for the poor guy, I made soothing noises, and said I understood, and these things could happen. Then he blurted out that he'd never laid a woman yet, because he could never get a hard-on, and it was so damned unfair, because he could always get a hard-on when he wanted to jerk off.

"I was really sorry for him. He was such a nice guy, kind and gentle and fun to be with. I ought to say is, because he's still all those things, and we've been having it off regularly now for nearly two years. I would marry him, I think, but he says no, because he's afraid something else might happen to him and he might be permanently impotent, which wouldn't be good for me or him if we were married, but like we are, if he can't perform, he can just disappear without any fuss.

"Well, as I say, I was feeling real sorry for him, and all my mothering instincts were coming welling up, and so I took him in my arms, and practically saying, 'There, there, little boy, it'll soon be better.' I didn't say that, of course, and I can't remember now exactly what I did say, but it had that sort of meaning. As I soothed him I ran my hand up and down his spine and over his buttocks. Whenever I touched his buttocks, he seemed to push his cock against me, as if I'd touched a nerve. So I stayed with his buttocks, and ran my hand lightly backwards and forwards over them.

"Then all of a sudden I felt his cock coming up hard against my thigh, and I did not stop caressing his buttocks until I felt it jerk once or twice. Believe me, Dr. Chartham, up to that point I had been the most unturned off woman in the world, as dry as a bone, and without a sexual thought in my head except the unhappy limpness of Tristan's poor cock. But as soon as I felt that rock-hard weapon jerking against my thigh, my clit and cunt were all on fire.

"He didn't seem to realise what had happened, until I said, 'Honey, come in me quick, I'm nearly coming.' 'Ha, ha! Very funny!' he sort of snapped, so I took my hand and put it on his cock. 'Jeeze!' he shouted, and I mean shouted, and I thought he was going to hit the ceiling. But he was on me before I knew what was happening and I helped him in and he began to buck away. He'd probably bucked three or four times when I came off the first time, and he kept grinding away, and I came again. Then I put down my hands and began to stroke his buttocks, and within seconds he shot off, and I kept stroking his buttocks, and he kept bucking until he whispered, 'Lay off, honey, please!' And I said, 'Lay off what?' And he said, 'Stroking my ass.' So I stopped and he stopped bucking, and lay on top of me, panting and his heart racing so hard he couldn't speak.

"When he quieted down, he got off me, and began to kiss me wildly. 'Jeeze, that was great! At last I've fucked a woman and it was great, and I'm glad it was you, because I like you better than any woman I know. What did you do to me?' 'I just stroked your ass,' I said. 'That's all, and then your cock was as horny as a stallion with three on-heat mares prancing round him, all wanting it.' 'And so long as you went on stroking I couldn't stop fucking. I thought I was going through the top of my head. Do you think it will happen again?' So I suggested we had a smoke and a drink and tried again in a while.

"So that's what we did, and it happened again, and the hornier he got, the hornier I got. I've been around a bit, but those lays are my most memorable ones. 'Christ, what do you think is the matter with me?' 'I don't know,' I said, 'and I wouldn't worry. If you can get a hard-on and get as horny as you do by having a girl stroke your ass, what's it matter what is the matter with you?' 'But it's not normal,' he said. 'But its results are bloody great,' I said. 'I think you're a witch,' he said, holding me hard in his arms and kissing me. 'The greatest witch in the world.'

"Well, having found out what would turn him on, and send me wild at the same time, I suppose because I felt I had a special sort of power over him, we next discovered that I could give him head, and do all those other sort of natural things to him, just so long as I kept one hand, not necessarily two, gently stroking his buttocks. In the past, and I still am, I had always been turned on by watching a guy's cock gradually getting hard. One of the ways in which I can be turned on so wild it's not true with Tristan is by making him stand in front of a mirror. We have to stand sideways because he's too tall for me to see over his shoulder. I stand behind him, and stroke his buttocks with both hands, and by degrees his cock begins to get hard. If I rub my nipples lightly against his back while I'm doing this, I can bring myself off by the time he's got fully hard. If I go on stroking his buttocks after he's got hard, he'll come off after a time, just like he will if he's in me, not moving, and I stroke his buttocks. It all sounds crazy I know, and if you don't believe me, I'm sure Tristan wouldn't refuse to give you a demonstration. But I don't think you'll ever find better evidence for what you are saying, 'We are all sexual individuals.' I don't know whether you'll be able to use this. Tristan says he doesn't mind, so long as you don't identify either of us."

* * * *

I believe that there is very little a couple can do sexually with one another that is perverted or deviant, or whatever you like to call it, but that the natural conclusion of fucking is coming off with the penis in the vagina. If you like to bring one another off in other ways every now and again, that's perfectly OK. *It's only when you can't come off by penis-vagina contact that you lay yourself open to charges of perversion.* Even so, I can't really find it in my heart to condemn this. Everyone is entitled to the sexual experience, and for me it is immaterial how they obtain it. I, nevertheless, think that orgasm with the penis in the vagina is the most certain way for the partners to express the depth of their emotional love for one another.

Footnote on Fetishism

I don't want to make a full chapter out of fetishism, so I'll slip it in here.

What fetishism really is, is not fully understood by most people. (I hate to use the word "normal" in any sexual context, but I must use it here.) Normally, both men and women are aroused by seeing each other's body as a whole. However, some people become focused on one part of the body and can only respond sexually to seeing that part—head hair, feet, buttocks, fingers—while others respond to objects which have nothing to do with the partner's body, especially underclothing (panties, stockings, garters, girdle, bra) and shoes, boots, leather, long gloves, rubber, and so on. Unless they can observe these parts of the body and other objects, or wear or have the partner wear their peculiar fetishistic article of clothing, they cannot be sexually aroused and reach orgasm.

I know a man who can only get an erection and come off if his partner is nude except for a feather boa and a string of pearls, while another friend of mine can only respond likewise if he is wearing frilly lace panties with an opening through which his penis can protrude. A client once sought my help because he could only be roused if he wore a nylon raincoat and Wellington boots.

All right, these people are kinky! And all right, so what?

Everyone is entitled to the experience of sex, and if, because of some psychological quirk, they can only have this experience by stimulating themselves by the use of their fetish, they are absolutely justified in doing so. Unfortunately, most fetishists have to go to prostitutes for their relief, since it is difficult for them to find other partners who will accept their fetishistic needs. (My friends of the feather boa and frilly panties are lucky because they explained their needs to their wives before marriage, and the wives were intelligent enough to humor their harmless aids. My client had not been so fortunate, and his marriage was on the verge of breaking up, because his new young wife was horrified, not so much by the nylon raincoat and Wellington boots, as by the state of mind that needed the wearing of these things to achieve erection.)

I think that the general attitude of women toward fetishists in the past has been unfortunate, because to become accustomed to the use of a fetish by the partner, unless it is very way out, is not difficult. However, women do have a certain excuse, because there are practically no women fetishists, and never have been. I asked the question because I wondered whether the development of female sexuality had released formerly suppressed fetishistic tendencies.

The short answer is: not one of the 198 was a fetishist according to the definition I have given above. But I think it would be useful to conclude this note with a comment by Charlotte of London, England.

"I see no harm in anything that encourages arousal and anyone, particularly the male, who finds some material or object that can stimulate them to a more than ordinary response, should be encouraged to indulge themselves, always bearing in mind that it should be with a willing and cooperative partner."

My sentiments entirely!

4

The Hard Stuff

I AM NOT going to enter the lists of those who attempt to define pornography. Literally, it comes from two Greek words which mean "the writing of harlots"; it is, therefore, first and foremost sexually arousing material, either written or in pictures or photographs or films or "live" shows, which depicts basic sexual activities. Personally, I can find nothing intellectually or aesthetically objectionable in visual pornography of any kind, though there is some written pornography that has come my way that tends to turn me off.

I believe it to be a fact of life, that except for certain neurotics, there is no male who is not sexually aroused by pornography of any kind. It is up to each individual to decide for himself, whether or not he wants to read or look at pornography. It is equally a fact of life, that there are some who have discovered that only by the use of pornography of one kind or another can they have a satisfying sexual experience. This is a pity, but in accordance with my attitude to any other sex-aid, I believe it should be made available for them. My only reservation about pornography is that it should be kept out of reach of young children who could get from it a wrong impression of what sex and love is all about, and condition them for life from responding to physical sex as the expression of emotional love and affection.

Anyone who has been in a men's public loo will know from the large diversity of sexually erotic and pornographic graffiti which cover its walls, that this desire of the male to leave behind him a crude sexual expression is a fairly widespread male behavior feature. But women also know that the walls of their public loos are not so decorated, or only slightly so decorated.

On this point, Kinsey says that only 25 percent of female graffiti investigated by him were sexual—either written or drawn—and that most of the rest referred to love, and what drawings there were, were mostly hearts. In comparison, 86 percent of all male graffiti was devoted to three main subjects: male and female genitalia; genital, oral, or anal activity (both "straight" and "gay"), and "vernacular vocabularies which, by association, are erotically significant for most males."

On the basis of this difference between male and female display of interest in pornographic graffiti, it has long been held that women are not, on the whole, responsive to pornography. In support of this, it has been pointed out that the vast bulk of written and visual pornography is produced for a male readership or audience, that the audiences at "blue" films, "live" shows, and other visual displays are nearly always exclusively male.

I have doubted this for some time. I have believed that men have somehow got it into their heads that women must be protected from the ultrasordidness of most pornography, and have actually prevented women from joining audiences at visual shows. While it is true that I have never seen more than one or two women in audiences made up of several dozen males at the "live" shows and "blue" films I have attended—about two dozen—and while it is true that I have yet to see a woman at any minor "blue" film show either in America or this country, anyone who saw a performance of *Deep Throat* in New York recently must have been struck by the large number of women in the audience. It is equally true, in my experience, that women today attend private "blue" film showings and appear to be as appreciative as the men, in fact are as appreciative. So is anything happening?

I have, in the past, heard the argument that if women felt a need for or were even capable of response to pornography, being barred from associating with men in this activity, they would have produced their own pornography. This they have not done, and why? Because not having the same response to psychological stimuli that men have they have not felt the need for it.

So what are these women doing at "live" shows and "blue" film sessions and obviously enjoying them? Does it mean that because they are now better understanding and developing their own sexuality, they have discovered that they can respond to pornography and with good effect? It was to throw some light on this that I asked the question: Are you aroused by pornography of any kind?

Here's a revelation!

Of our 198 women, 27 have never read a pornographic book or seen any visual pornography; and 41 have had experience of pornography in one form or another and either have not been roused or have, on the contrary, been turned off. The remaining 130 (a little more than two-thirds) have read, or seen visual, pornography and been definitely roused by it.

I feel this to be encouraging to my suggestion that woman's response to pornography in the past has been stifled, and that her burgeoning sexuality is awakening her to sexual experiences which, previously, she was unaware that she could have.

Here is what a few of them say about their responses to pornography, which are typical of many others.

* * * *

"Pornography is fairly new to me, and though I am still not completely turned on by the blue films I've seen, I'm finding the erotic effect to be increasing. I realised something that was interesting to me after watching the last movie. I had an urge to prove that I could have been even more exciting and stimulating than the woman we had seen on the screen. Our lovemaking after viewing the film was highly satisfying to both me and my lover."

* * * *

"My response to pornography depends on my mood. My dependency needs extend to what I call my 'rape syndrome.' In certain moods the harsh shock of pornography can, therefore, turn me on. Otherwise the sight of a cunt as big as a house is too big a shock. I've seen few films besides the one which depicted this last, but I find that I have to make an initial adaptation to the ferocity of it, then the sordid aspect begins to grow on me, but it's somehow secondhand.

"I don't think I would get turned on very much by watching a 'live' show. I like to get, and do get, totally involved in lovemaking. Growing up for me meant this realisation that it wasn't worth sleeping with people I didn't care about emotionally, because not only was I missing this sphere of involvement, but I also couldn't let myself go fully physically."

* * * *

"Not all pornography rouses me, but some does. One example stands out in my mind. A little while ago I went to stay with a friend whose husband had just been killed. They hadn't been married long. One day I was alone in the apartment and was straightening up her bedroom when I found a box containing some Polaroid photos of my friend and her husband in various stages of undressing, and there were many nude photos of both of them. The camera must have had an automatic shutter because there were many pictures of them engaged in all kinds of sexual activities. A high percentage showed acts of oral sex, and most of these were of my friend fellating her husband. Looking at them, I became extremely aroused. After that, whenever I was alone in the apartment, I would get them out and look at them again. Sometimes I even masturbated while I was looking at them."

* * * *

"Books have a terrific effect—the harder the porn the better. I am roused by both written and photographic material—either heterosexual, or male homosexual, but not lesbian. Blue films have a slight effect provided I am with someone who is personally important to me. I wouldn't have the courage to go to a 'live' show, for fear of being recognised."

* * * *

"Yes, all pornography turns me on, but live shows. I've never seen one and have never had a desire to see one. Too embarrassing."

* * * *

"I found some of this in my brother's room, showing people fucking and doing other things to one another. *I learned a whole lot about sex from this stuff.* Some of it showed girls not much older than me [she's 16] getting fucked by boys the same age. That turned me on, believe me. The pictures of

hem playing with each other turn me on, too, most
of all the ones where they are doing it to each other
with their mouths."

To be aware of oral sex, and responding to it in
adolescence, is surely going to show dividends,
in the lack of inhibitions, for the rising generation.

* * * *

"The most super blue film I ever saw (in Den-
mark, of course) showed a superman being tied
down by three girls, having his clothes cut off him
while spreadeagled on a bed, and being devoured
by the girls. I don't know how many times I came
off without touching myself while watching this
film."

* * * *

"I like reading and am roused by any sort of
porn. And I have to admit that I would love to see
a blue film, or, even more a live show between two
males, or two females, or two men and two women
(a foursome!)"

* * * *

"Only good photos turn me on, especially of
nude males, front view, with large, low-hanging
balls. Anything of a woman alone turns me right
off."

* * * *

"Written porn with some well-done pictures
quickly makes me feel horny. Heavy detailed de-

scriptions of feelings or acts between a man and a woman or two women. Descriptions of how the woman feels. I have never seen a blue film or a live show, but would like to see one involving women or woman and man."

* * * *

"I think any normally sexually oriented person cannot fail to be stimulated by porn to some degree. I find it good for me personally just as a stimulus. I like reading or looking at it with a male partner. It's very arousing to see him gradually getting a hard-on, and this, in those circumstances, probably stimulates me more than the actual porn itself."

Remember! It's a woman speaking!

5

Master and Slave

--◦--❯-❯◦❮-❮--◦--

Kinsey gives the following comparative figures for erotic response to sadomasochistic stories:

Erotic response	By females	By males
	%	%
Definite and/or frequent	3	10
Some response	9	12
Never	88	78

He then goes on to say:

That fewer of the females and more of the males had responded, appears again to have depended on the fact that reactions to sadomasochistic stories rely on fantasy. As many females as males seem to react erotically when they are bitten or when they engage in more specifically sadomasochistic contacts, and this further emphasizes the differences in the psychologic reactions of the two sexes.*

Kinsey, *Sexual Behavior in the Human Female*, p. 677.

A little later he goes on to point out that four times as many women react to being bitten as had reacted to sadomasochistic stories, while only twice as many men had so reacted. I wonder if there is any significance in this, e.g., has the woman's subservient role in sex conditioned her more to masochism than sadism? Yet, a cursory survey I made recently of advertisements in contact magazines revealed as many advertisements from women offering "discipline" as from men seeking "governesses." I doubt, however, whether any value can be placed on this, because the advertisements offering "discipline" may have been inserted by prostitutes, whose fee is always larger than usual for participating in sadomasochistic acts.

Usually women are thought of as gentle creatures, and so, for the most part, they are. But do they have secret yearnings to be cruel or to be purged of their guilt for being a woman by submitting to cruelty inflicted on them? Hence, my questions about sexual arousal in response to sadomasochism.

The disclosures made by my collaborators couldn't have pleased me more!

Three-quarters (139) rejected both sadism and masochism as a means of sexual arousal out of hand. I love you all, because I am a gentle man and could not ever inflict any kind of pain on a woman. Nor do I wish any of you to inflict pain on me.

(Something has just occurred to me. I have a very high threshold of pain. I can have a tooth

tracted, for example, without even a local anes-
etic and suffer nothing more than a slight dis-
omfort. This helped me a great deal during World
War II, when, captured by the Gestapo, I came
rough torture by them three times without break-
g. But—at both my schools I was mercilessly
eaten frequently by sadistic headmasters. At my
ublic school [private high school] I was so badly
eaten by my headmaster, at least once a fortnight,
at my behind would be so raw I could not sit
own for several days. According to the "trick-
yclists" this ought to have made me a sexual maso-
hist, but I'm not. [I don't very much care for being
tten, though I do like my buttocks squeezed hard,
st as I'm coming.] I hated that ghastly little fat man
ntil he died two or three years ago at the age of
nety. But if he helped me to resist the Gestapo
rture, perhaps I ought to be a little bit grateful.
's strange how something new crops up every
y!)

As for those who admit to sadistic and masochistic
tivities, none of them is involved in anything
ally nasty. The nastiest, in fact, turn out to be
ntasists, like this one.

"Yippa. Having, in my fantasy, spreadeagled
y lovely man on the bed, naked, of course, I then
hip him and cane him, and eventually tie up his
ick and balls so that he can't move without giv-
g himself immense pain. Then somehow, I turn
m over and insert various prick-shaped objects
to his rear-hole, while he yells and screams, and,

of course, wriggles deliciously. Then I shave off a
his body hair, and dress him in a waistcoat, sock
and boots, and make him crawl about the floor wit
his genitals exposed for my pleasure. As I glo.
over them I masturbate violently till I come off.
have no masochistic desires, either real or fantasy."

The actual sadistic and masochistic acts indulge
in are all much milder than this fantasy. For ex
ample—

"I have tied up several lovers so that they can
escape my caresses. Then I lick them all over, grad
ually building up their excitement. When the
seem about to come, I stop and wait till they'v
cooled down. Then I begin again and stop. I do th
until they are writhing and begging for mercif
release. But I won't give them that until I thin
they've deserved it. I don't think of this as sadistic
I'm not inflicting any pain. It arouses me tremen
dously and when I decide to let them come, I brin
them off by rubbing their cocks between my sex
lips. I always come as soon as I feel their seme
spurting.

"As for masochistic acts: One of my lovers pre
tended to rape me once. I enjoyed this immensely
I've never been spanked so I don't know if the actu
ality would arouse me as thinking about it doe
I'd like to try it, tho'. During cunnilingus I enjo
being bitten on my inner thighs—never on m
actual sex-lips—and I often ask for this. The bite
are painful, but I crave them, tho' I'm bruised fo
days afterwards. I'm inclined to think that th

186

craving is not so much masochistic as a need for deeper, more intense stimulation at that point in lovemaking."

Or—

"I get turned on by one thing—I baby-sit. One family I sit for has a nine-year-old boy who is a brat. His parents told me I should punish him like they do when he does something wrong. They told him he has to let me, or his father will punish him worse when they get home. They spank him and they said I should, too. But I spank his bare behind. His father just clouts him. Every time I have to spank him for something he does, and I think the brat does it deliberately because he gets a hard-on every time. Spanking him makes me terribly randy, and afterwards I have to go to the loo and jerk myself off. I can't tell whether he comes while I'm spanking him, but he doesn't ejaculate. Can boys of nine come? I watched him once sort of jerking himself off in the bath when he didn't know I was watching. When you're sixteen you sometimes think you know it all, but gosh, you don't know hardly anything. By the way, being hurt turns me right off."

Or—

"He plays a form of sadism with me, and I pretend submissiveness—but not sexually. He loves to make appointments and break them at the last moment and sometimes I rebel, but most of the time I recognise that it is his way, and since I cannot change him, I have to accept it. But then, just when

I think perhaps it is his way of breaking off with me, he does something generous and kind and loving and then I know he's just been putting me in what he considers the proper perspective. Business and his family come first, and then I fit somewhere in the picture. If accepting this is masochistic on my part, I'm glad."

Or—

"I am a mild masochist—nothing more than a spanking or being put down as a 'mere' woman. I do not believe in Women's Lib. I want Man to dominate me!"

Or—

"*Sadistic acts, masochistic acts, fetishes.* I don't really know which of these categories these fit into, so I'll just write what we like.

"(i) We sometimes whip each other with a belt. I can come off like that, but he can't.

"(ii) I suck him to a certain point and won't let him come. Then if he wants to come he has to wank himself off. I find watching him do this really rouses me. When he spurts, I press my fingers hard on my clit and I'm away, too.

"(iii) He gets me to the point-of-no-return and then won't let me have his cock inside me to satisfy me. I have to finish myself off, then he kneels astride me and wanks himself and spurts all over my belly. Before he has time to go soft, he goes in me, and fucks me really violently till he comes again. I come two or three times while he is doing this. Sometimes nearly half-an-hour goes by before he can shoot off again. He's flat out for a couple of hours afterwards, which gives me pleasure because I can satisfy him so much."

Or—

"*Sadistic acts*. Only once have I gained pleasure from this. I knew a particularly 'doormat' type of boy who unfortunately 'fell in love' with me. I became really sick of his nonstop attention, and one day, when we were staying with friends of his, I asked him to lie down on the floor. The silly bugger did just that. Then for no reason I just kicked him. He didn't make any effort to stop me, and I found I was enjoying it. Then all of a sudden I came, and the fun went out of it, so I stopped. I would never do it again. It frightened me. I don't like being hurt myself."

Or—

"Along with my desire to feel a man's bottom, I sometimes have the urge to spank it. Several of my lovers with really beautiful bottoms have let me do this. I don't do it hard, but it arouses me so much, he has to come in me immediately, and often he hasn't got in properly before I've come."

Or—

"I do like to make men suffer psychologically. It rouses me to sexually rouse a man and then turn cold towards him. When I was younger, I did this by passionately kissing and embracing a boy until he was very excited, and then, when he tried to go further, I would slap him and pretend to be angry with him. Now I do it in much more subtle ways.

For instance, if a man I think is sexy is paying me a lot of attention, I act very friendly at first. Then when he thinks he is getting somewhere with me, I start to be less and less friendly and pay less and less attention to him. At the same time I wear sexier clothes and act sexier. This is only a little game I play sometimes, but it does rouse me sexually."

All cock-teasers are sadists, though they may be playing "only little games."

6

Doing Your Own Thing

·············➤>◦<◄·············

ANYONE WHO DEALS with people's sexual difficulties will tell you that sexually we are all, each one of us, sexual individuals—despite the fact that we may, on the face of it, follow certain general patterns. I've been in this business of counseling for more than forty years now, and the longer I go on doing it, the more I know I have to learn. This is why I asked my final question: Are you sexually roused by anything else that I haven't listed?

Ladies, you've taught me a thing or two. Here is a selection of the more interesting.

*   *   *   *

"I get very turned on by watching him being chatted up and being groped by another man, and seeing that he is getting very worked up, and yet knowing that he will come to me.

191

* * * *

"Doing things in semipublic. Oral sex in a church parking lot on Sunday. Manual sex under a coat at concerts where everyone is sitting on the floor. Making love in the bedroom while the staid couple who own the place are in the room next to yours, thinking you are in the kitchen having a snack. And, with people I don't know too well, I like to instill in them doubts as to which sex I really prefer so they start to wonder about me. I guess I'm a sort of closet exhibitionist."

* * * *

"Some of my girlfriends and I play sex games that turn us all on. We play one where we ask each other real personal questions about sex, and what we've done with boys. If a girl refuses to answer or another girl catches her lying she has to pay a penalty. The first time she just has to take some clothes off. When we're all naked the game gets good.

"We have penalties like having to stand naked in front of an open window, or having to suck another girl's tits or having to kiss her behind or having to play with yourself while the other girls watch. We're always trying to think of new penalties.

"We play strip poker, too. I played that once with my boyfriend and another couple. That really turned me on. I get turned on a whole bunch by letting a boy I like see me naked or part-naked. I think I have a good figure for sixteen. I wear a 34 bra with a B cup, my waist is 22, and my hips are 34. I get turned on by looking at myself in the mirror when I'm naked and feeling my body.

"I have a real small bikini I wear when I go swimming. It turns me on to see the boys watching me. A boyfriend of mine has a swimming pool at his house. Once when we were there alone, I took off my bikini and went skinny dipping. That turned us both on a whole bunch. It's the only time yet I've fucked in water. It was fantastic. We both blew our minds, though he came too soon for my liking. I suppose he was over excited."

* * * *

"One thing that rouses me is being watched while I'm undressing or nude. It arouses me to see a man becoming aroused by watching me undress or by watching me when I'm nude. If he is already undressed himself, it arouses me to see his penis become erect as I undress. I also get aroused when a man takes Polaroid photos of me when I'm partially undressed or nude. I like to make it a part of our lovemaking.

"Another thing that rouses me is watching a man masturbate. On a very few occasions I have seen another woman masturbating, and that has aroused me, too. I also like to watch myself in a mirror when I masturbate.

"In some cases, seeing a nude woman or a photo of a nude woman is arousing to me. She has to be exceptionally beautiful, though. I get especially roused if her breasts and bottom are very well shaped and if her skin is smooth and silky. One final thing that arouses me is sunbathing in the nude. I do it whenever I get a chance, and afterwards, I'm usually so aroused that I go back to my room and masturbate."

* * * *

"This is something that only turns me on with my 'virgin.' I make him put on my clothes and tights. Then I put make-up on him and you can hardly tell the difference between him and a girl. It's only his big feet that spoil the effect. Just kissing him when he's like that makes me very randy.

"The other thing is erotic phone calls. I first tried one for a laugh. I knew a guy who had three extensions to his phone. I picked an evening when he had some friends in. I phoned and masturbated at the same time. Then without warning I came. The result was quite interesting. The three guys who had been listening decided to do the same, and we spent the rest of the call talking sex and having orgasms all over the place.

"I gave up doing it with the guys, and now only do it with my girlfriend. What my imagination does do on these calls! Unfortunately we can't do it very often, as we have to wait until both sets of parents are out at the same time.

"I really don't know how I would get on without my girlfriend. Guys are great, but I just couldn't do without her."

* * * *

"Romantic words and stories by the other partner. Him telling me how he would have loved to have taken me first at fourteen, when I lost my virginity. How he seduced his girlfriends, and how he himself was made love to by an older girl when he was only fourteen. The spoken word at the right time can conjure up beautiful thoughts and ideas. However, any mention of my past men, or trying to encourage me to talk, makes me think inward, and I start to recall events, which needs concentration. Then I lose my mood, which takes a lot of regaining."

* * * *

"Surprise attack, being taken usually from behind, with no preliminaries other than the brisk removal of lower garments. Lubrication is nearly instantaneous and freer than more prolonged foreplay produces, and the presence of other interested people, especially if they are enjoying sex at the same time, and making a bit of noise about it."

* * * *

"I am thirty. Divorced ten years. One daughter. I have had a boyfriend for over four years whom I live with on weekends only. I love him very much but we are not going to marry, because he is not prepared to be tied down. However, sexually he is faithful (or within 99 percent anyway!)

"Although I really love him, sometimes he is *not* everything I want in bed. He is very conservative. Lights out, etc., never kisses me below the waist, never says anything sexy, but still he nearly always satisfies me, because it's a more involved thing than just physical sensation. It's love as well.

"So sometimes I'm unfaithful, with a man who knows everything about sex, and I enjoy every minute. But I have no emotional feelings for him, so I am utterly selfish. I believe that by being occasionally unfaithful and satisfying the animal desires and that pure lust that we all have, I can love my boyfriend more than ever because I am not frustrated, and I can have an enormous respect for him as he is a very honest and straight man.

"I could wish he'd be a bit more romantic and adventurous, and just once I'd like to have him hit me, but he never would. Sometimes he bites me in his passion, and afterwards, he is truly upset for hurting me. He can't understand that I don't mind at all, that in fact, I want him to let himself go."

* * * *

"Anything else . . . are you ready?

"(a) Anything I do with my body in preparation for lovemaking is arousing to me. This includes the usual washing and perfuming. I have one perfume I apply *only* before lovemaking. I have associated this particular scent with pleasure to the extent that if I should smell the scent on another woman, perhaps in an elevator, or on the bus, my clitoris starts to throb!

"Also, I occasionally write pornographic statements (graffiti) on my body with a marking pen.

While doing this, I am turned on by the thought of my lover uncovering these little phrases.

"(b) Often (but not so often as to get boring) I insert a lifesaver candy or mint high into my vagina several hours before lovemaking. Just anticipating his tasting the different flavor is enough to make me start secreting enough juice so that by the time he's going down on me, the full flavor is detectable and the candy is half melted.

"(c) I am *very* stimulated by going out with my lover without panties or without clothes entirely except for shoes and trenchcoat. He delights in knowing that only we two know about my nakedness, and I am almost feverishly excited. I usually casually mention my pantyless or clothesless state whilst we are in a restaurant. This is exciting to us both, as he immediately gets an erection and, again, *no one knows* save us! I should add that I was doing this long before Joan Garrity ever wrote *The Sensuous Woman!*

"(d) One of the most exciting sex acts, to me, and not always—I hate to get in a rut!—is to have my lover enter my mouth from above. Thus, while I am fellating him, I am also the passive partner. This is exquisitely exciting if he holds my hands so that I can indulge my bondage fantasy. Legman refers to this active-male, passive-female fellatio as "irrumation." I find it true that if the female is sexually aroused, her gag reflex will diminish—for while I can never take his full length when he's on his back and I am fellating him, I find that I can take his

197

full seven and a half inches with no problem when he's actively thrusting into me . . . and it's his dominance that turns me on so.

"(e) I've been tied up by two different men—but they weren't able to enjoy it as much as I'd hoped, and thus, while it was exciting to me, it wasn't so great as I think it could be. These men were rather passive, and it was as if once they had me all open and available and helpless, they didn't quite know what to do about it!

"(f) Writing and receiving erotic letters (including this one!), especially those I write to my lover. I can get myself very excited very quickly while seeing my own sexy words flow onto paper."

Conclusions:
"A Word in Your Ear, Lady!"

A SHORT TIME ago, I began research on the nature of the human sex-drive in which I had the collaboration of 372 couples who were either married or were living together in a continuing relationship. As part of my scheme to try to find out what made us tick sexually, each of the couples kept a diary in which they wrote down in detail every sexual activity in which they took part, either together or singly, for a period of one month.

From the material, it emerged that the great majority of people make love more frequently in response to the promptings of their "voluntary" sex-drive than to their "involuntary" sex-drive. That is to say, they deliberately turned on to, or allowed themselves to be turned on by psychological stimuli more often than they were turned on by physiological stimuli. They put their sexual imaginations to work in order to have a sexual experience rather than wait for the chemicals in their bodies to regulate their sexual activity.

I don't say that this was a shattering new discovery (you can read all about it for yourselves in my book *Your Sex-Drive*), but it had never been brought out and presented to the lay public, and the professionals had mostly tended to overlook it, too. There were some cries of disbelief from them, but mostly silence, I think because they had not taken it more seriously into consideration themselves.

I've got to admit that I was quite excited myself when I realized this did happen to the majority of people, but what really impressed itself on me was the fact that the women among my collaborators were as sexually imaginative and, it followed, as responsive to psychological stimuli as men allegedly --and, in fact—are. It was this realization that made me set in motion this investigation.

As I've said, until you must be sick of hearing me say so, I have been counseling men and women with sexual difficulties of one kind or another for over forty years. When you do this job conscientiously —and you have no business doing it if you're not conscientious—you try to keep up with all the latest developments and discoveries in the field of how sexuality works. I think we—counselors and others —are all aware that our knowledge of human sexuality, of how we tick sexually, has been very far from complete and is still very far from complete. When we have delved into unknown territory in the past—because men have predominated in this field of research, and, I suppose, because men are innately selfish—we have concentrated more on the study of the male than of the study of the female. (Kinsey was the first to give *equal* consideration to both.)

But besides adding to the male's awareness of what he was capable of sexually by what we discovered, we ignored the female, I am sure, because we were still laboring under the impression, accentuated, I believe, by the nature of her traditional sex role of passive partner, that her sexuality, if she had any in her own right at all, was inferior to the male's.

That this was not necessarily so ought to have struck me much earlier than it did—in the early sixties—when I was prompted to write *Mainly for Wives* by a scandal which overtook one of our new towns, involving the women on the great modern estates there popping into bed with the milkman, the baker, the window-cleaner, and the grocery boy. If they did this, it seemed to me that they had good reason, and the only reason could be that their own partners were failing them sexually. So I decided to encourage them to take an equal share in the sexual responsibilities of their marriages, and to change their traditional sex-role of hunted to that of huntress whenever they felt like it.

Even then, it did not occur to me that women were far more like men in their sexual responsiveness than anyone had ever imagined. Yet it ought to have struck me, because by this time I had been married for thirty years to a woman who most definitely did have a sexuality that equalled mine in all respects. I had joyfully accepted this, and so readily, too, that I selfishly did not give a thought to others. I think that if I had given a thought to it at all, I would have believed that we were a unique couple.

Now I am convinced that if we were unique, we need not have been. The emergence from sexual purdah which more and more women have taken part in over the last five years, though by no means yet complete, has shown me that we should have been one couple in millions.

Women are sexual beings in their own right. If I seem to be stating a truism, it will appear so only to the converted. And believe me, among men there is only one convert in millions.

Women have a sexuality which over the last century and more has been stifled not only by her chauvinist male, but by herself. When men do admit this sexuality, they will not admit that it is on a par with theirs. If, they say, women had anything approaching male sexuality, not necessarily in nature, but in quality, why for heaven's sake do they have all this difficulty in coming off and why is there all this fuss about it?

Ladies, please accept the fact that you have a sexuality! Please wake it up if it is asleep! Please encourage it by every means you know to develop and flower! Remember that your interest and your excitement are powerfully stimulating to your lovers. Enjoy them, while you enjoy yourselves. There are strong indications liberally scattered throughout all the foregoing pages that the woman's responses to sex are not only as strong as the male's, but that they are identical in many of their aspects. I believe that when we know all about female sexuality we shall not be able to differentiate it from male sexuality in a single important particular.

Author's Note

May I express my grateful thanks to all the women who have helped me so magnificently in making this little study possible. I think you will find, as time goes by, that you have struck a blow for women's sexual liberty that is far more effective than you think it is going to be at the moment.

Appendix

—•—>—•—>—•—<—•—<—•—•—

Without Comment

Dear Sir,

In answer to your request what turns women on, I send you my letter on full approval of my husband.

First of all we are a happy married couple of 20 yrs I am 45 yrs of age and Chris is 59 yrs old, 1. My husband is a marvlous lover and seducer very broad and tall, he is very handsome and one of the things I got mad for his the mass of hair on his belly and chest.

I love to dangle my breasts over his body over is hairy parts, (this he loves to) 2. Secondly no matter what any women say as regards of the male cock, every one likes her mate to own a big one.

When my husband stands naked his prick hangs 6½ inches when limp, on the erection it stiffens rock hard to 8¼ inches and when I say hard at that size I mean it.

When we were courting and were out in the car petting he thought I would stop him because of the size, but when I felt it in the dark my heart beat with joy, so I sat over him and asked him to put the light on for me to see it.

And I took every ince of his 8¼ size cock with a blob of jelly, and I was a virgin.

3. Thirdly, we practise oral love, he would rather tongue my fanny, and put his knob up than be sucked of, I only take it in my mouth to relieve him when I am on my periods.

4. Fourthly. We make love anywhere, on the couch, on the floor, on a chair straddling, bending of a chair up against the wall but mostly the bedroom.

5. Fifthly, we like to be watched without the other person knowing it, as we have to single lodgers in the bedroom next to ours, I found when cleaning the picture on the wall a big hole and looking through saw my husband lying in bed and below the wash basin a mike putting it by my hear I could hear every noise from our bedroom.

I told my husband and we agreed to give them something worth seeing now we lie on the top of the bed with the light on. My husband tells me I'm going get fucked and waves his horse cock over my twat touching the cliteros.

We get stared at in the mornings but if only they new.

6. Sixth, We make love with mirrors I watch it

going in, then I sit on my husband and he watches it going in but it makes him come to fast.

Our favorite way is me lying on the top when its up Chris arches his back and I ride his big cock it helps me to come faster.

Well, there you are these are the things that turn me on. hope they help you in your research,

                                        Yours Sincerely,

from

PENTHOUSE/Ballantine

THE SENSUOUS COUPLE,
Robert Chartham

The best-seller by Britain's foremost sexologist reveals the simple things every couple can do together to bring the greatest pleasure and enjoyment to each other.

$1.25

WHAT TURNS WOMEN ON,
Robert Chartham

These women in letters to a sympathetic and qualified friend have discussed in their own graphic and sometimes startling words, their more intimate desires. One thing becomes very clear—there is a lot more that turns women on than might have been expected.

$1.50

SUPER MARRIAGE-SUPER SEX,
H. F. Freedman

A handbook for people who already know about sex—and want to learn more. A good sex relationship is basic to a good marriage, and it is clear that "good" means totally accepting.

$1.50

Ballantine Books in Psychology

━━━━━━━━━━━━━━━━━━━━━━━

TRANSACTIONAL ANALYSIS IN PSYCHOTHERAPY
Eric Berne, M.D.

Dr. Berne first outlined the principles of transactional
analysis in this book. *Now a classic in the field.*

THE STRUCTURE AND DYNAMICS OF ORGANIZA-
TIONS AND GROUPS
Eric Berne, M.D.

Based on the principles of transactional analysis, this
book offers a systematic framework for the therapy of
"ailing" groups and organizations. *A "bold and cre-
ative" book.*

GAMES ALCOHOLICS PLAY
Claude Steiner

With a preface by Eric Berne, this book claims alcohol-
ism is not a disease and tells why treating an alcoholic
as a "sick" man may do him more harm than good.

BALLANTINE BOOKS
by Dr. Clark Moustakas

PSYCHOTHERAPY WITH CHILDREN: The Living Relationship, Clark Moustakas $1.65

Through verbatim dialogues of sessions with normal, gifted, handicapped, and disturbed children, the author takes the reader into the usually hidden world of the child at crucial moments of psychic development.

THE CHILD'S DISCOVERY OF HIMSELF, edited by Clark Moustakas $1.25

A superb collection of actual case studies of "alive" experiences of therapists working with children.

FROM
BALLANTINE BOOKS'
CHILD PSYCHOLOGY
SERIES

DIBS: In Search of Self, Virginia Axline $1.25

The deeply moving account of a disturbed child's successful struggle for identity. A rewarding experience for anyone who has—or ever expects to have—contact with children.

PLAY THERAPY, Virginia Axline $1.25

A landmark in its field, this work is a perceptive study of disturbed adolescents. *Contains actual drawings.*

The Politics of Experience

R. D. Laing

Given the conditions of contemporary civilization how can one claim that the "normal" man is sane?

In this famous book, a young British psychiatrist attacks the Establishment assumptions about "normality" with a radical and challenging view of the mental sickness built into our society . . .

"He has let us know. He has told us in such a way that we can not disregard it. . . . He speaks to no one but you and me."—Los Angeles Free Press

A BALLANTINE BOOK $.95